Making Goods
for
Villagers

Making Goods for Villagers

R.K. Agnihotri
Retd. Director General Police, M.P.

ALLIED PUBLISHERS PRIVATE LIMITED
New Delhi • Mumbai • Kolkata • Chennai • Nagpur
Ahmedabad • Bangalore • Hyderabad • Lucknow

ALLIED PULIBLISERS PRIVATE LIMITED

1/13-14 Asaf Ali Road, **New Delhi**–110002
Ph.: 011-23239001 • E-mail: delhi.books@alliedpublishers.com

47/9 Prag Narain Road, Near Kalyan Bhawan, **Lucknow**–226001
Ph.: 0522-2209942 • E-mail: lko.books@alliedpublishers.com

17 Chittaranjan Avenue, **Kolkata**–700072
Ph.: 033-22129618 • E-mail: cal.books@alliedpublishers.com

15 J.N. Heredia Marg, Ballard Estate, **Mumbai**–400001
Ph.: 022-42126969 • E-mail: mumbai.books@alliedpublishers.com

60 Shiv Sunder Apartments (Ground Floor), Central Bazar Road,
Bajaj Nagar, **Nagpur**–440010
Ph.: 0712-2234210 • E-mail: ngp.books@alliedpublishers.com

F-1 Sun House (First Floor), C.G. Road, Navrangpura,
Ellisbridge P.O., **Ahmedabad**–380006
Ph.: 079-26465916 • E-mail: ahmbd.books@alliedpublishers.com

751 Anna Salai, **Chennai**–600002
Ph.: 044-28523938 • E-mail: chennai.books@alliedpublishers.com

5th Main Road, Gandhinagar, **Bangalore**–560009
Ph.: 080-22262081 • E-mail: bngl.books@alliedpublishers.com

3-2-844/6 & 7 Kachiguda Station Road, **Hyderabad**–500027
Ph.: 040-24619079 • E-mail: hyd.books@alliedpublishers.com

Website: www.alliedpublishers.com

© R.K. Agnihotri

ISBN : 978-81-8424-674-2

First edition: 2011

Reprint 2012

Published by Sunil Sachdev and printed by Ravi Sachdev at Allied Publishers Pvt. Ltd.,
Printing Division, A-104 Mayapuri Phase II, New Delhi -110064

Foreword

The Economic Survey of India (2008–09), contains the following statements:

- While poverty rates have declined significantly, malnutrition has remained stubbornly high. Malnutrition, as measured by underweight children below three years of age, constitutes 45.9 per cent as per the National Family Health Survey 2005–06 (NFHS 3). It has also not significantly declined from its level of 47 per cent in 1998–99 (NFHS 2).

- It is evident that existing policies and programmes are not making a significant dent on malnutrition and need to be modified. While per capita consumption of cereals has declined, the share of non-cereals in food consumption has not grown to compensate for the decline in cereal availability.

The widespread hunger prevailing in our country is partly the result of inadequate purchasing power. Over 60 per cent of our population depends on farming for their livelihood. In the cultivated area, over 60 per cent depend on rainfall for the success of farming. In industrialised countries, 2 to 3 per cent of the population depends on agriculture for their job and income security. In contrast, in our country nearly two thirds of the population depends on crop and animal husbandry, forestry, fisheries, agro-processing and agri-business for their income. Often, rains fail and those dependent only on crops face serious problems in returning the credit they may have borrowed from institutional or private sources. Such indebtedness occasionally results in farmers' committing suicide. This is why, multiple sources of livelihood are important for income and livelihood security. Strengthening livelihoods and thereby saving lives is an urgent task.

Mahatma Gandhi diagnosed this need over 80 years ago when he wanted the starving people of Orissa to take to small scale industries, handicrafts and handlooms based on locally available raw material. For successful manufacture of goods in villages, it will be important to have backward linkages with technology and raw material and forward linkage with markets. There is a growing movement for organising Self Help Groups (SHGs) of women in villages based on micro-credit and micro-enterprises. Such SHGs become sustainable when assured and remunerative marketing is ensured.

There is a trend in our villages towards contract farming and manufacturing goods on the basis of specific brand names belonging to large companies. There is also scope for organising group enterprises, for example, through Food Parks, Biotechnology Parks, Information Technology Parks etc. The first and only Women's Biotechnology Park has been established at Siruseri village near Chennai. We need more initiatives of this kind. It is in this context, that the book "Making Goods for Villagers" provides excellent and implementable suggestions for augmenting rural income. The book shows the way for rural renaissance. We are grateful to Dr. R.K. Agnihotri for his labour of love for *Gram Swaraj*, which Gandhiji rightly emphasised, is the pathway to *Purna Swaraj*.

M.S. Swaminathan
Member of Parliament (Rajya Sabha)
Chairman, M.S. Swaminathan Research Foundation
Third Cross Street, Taramani Institutional Area
Chennai – 600 113 (India)
Email: swami@mssrf.res.in/msswami@vsnl.net

Preface

The concept of a self-sufficient village, which Gandhiji mooted during pre-independence struggle was perhaps, a part of his non-cooperation movement. But now in the 21st Century, this concept needs to be modified and the concept of a self sufficient village must be banished. Many industries have come up after the industrial revolution which benefit the masses of urban society but villagers lack the same.

This book *Making Goods for Villagers'* is inspired by my article under the same name, which was published in [Times of India, 1973] (see Appendix). This book deals with the problems of villagers, from a different point of view. Though the points mentioned may be criticised by some, a look on the necessities of the villagers and to have industries manufacturing goods especially for them is necessary. It was the industrial revolution of late 18th & 19th centuries, which enabled the developing nations of Europe to dominate the world.

The theme of "Making Goods for Villagers" is that the urban sector has to provide much greater support to the rural sector, far bigger in size and importance.

R.K. Agnihotri

Contents

Villages in the Pre-Industrial Revolution Era

1

The Times of India of the 2nd September, 1973 published an article written by myself bearing the title "MAKING GOODS FOR VILLAGERS". The same is included in this book as an Appendix. Picking up the central idea of this article after a gap of more than three decades, I set out to write my views on the fundamental strategy of development for rural India. I am aware this is, like swimming against the current in a fast flowing river.

Mahatma Gandhi mooted the idea of self-sufficient villages during the struggle for independence. Much water has flown down the holy Ganges since those times. In those days of early 20th century, a large number of industrial products were imported from England or other European countries. It was, perhaps, a part of his non-cooperation movement that he preached the denial of industrially produced goods for villagers. After the lapse of nearly a century, we find ourselves in a materially changed situation.

The idea of setting up small scale & cottage industries in villages has been a favorite theme of social workers and thinkers. They expect that the villagers can employ themselves gainfully, in these mini industrial units and thereby add to their income. While doing this, the industrial units in the villages will produce items of utility in the rural and urban areas. The concept gained a strong support from Mahatma Gandhi, who advocated the concept of self sufficient villages. In his scheme of things the villagers were expected to produce most of the items of their need within the village. If there is any surplus production, it is to be sold in the neighbouring villages or towns. In this concept the production of goods is to be on a small scale. In Mahatma Gandhi's view, the Charkha (or the spinning wheel) was the epitome of what shape the industry should take. In the ideal conditions contemplated by him, people will spin yarn needed by them from a Charkha and would get it woven into a cloth. This cloth, which came to be known as Khadi, became the symbol of the independence of the individual from any kind of regimentation. This eliminated the need of the situation, in which a large number of persons joined together, to work in a regimented manner for several hours every day, to produce goods. Large scale industries were not advocated by him. When he postulated this theory, India was under the British rule. This was not only political and administrative subjugation, taking away our civil rights but also much more. Being the leader of the Industrial Revolution, Britain flooded the Indian markets with goods produced by industries in Britain. This brought about an Economic slavery upon the Indian masses in addition to political subordination. Mahatma Gandhi took up the uprooting of the British Empire in India, from the very basic point of release from economic subjugation. The textile industry of Manchester and Birmingham had found a captive market in India. The Mahatma took up a very stormy campaign against the textiles exported from England. His Swadeshi movement led to large scale burning of clothes imported from England. Khadi became the ideal of our economic independence and Charkha its symbol.

This economic strategy was very appropriate for the conditions prevailing during the foreign rule. Even during this period, large scale textile industry took its birth in cities like Ahmedabad, Mumbai, Nagpur and several other cities. The urban population of our country started deriving all the advantages of mass production of goods. The idea of village industries, however, kept on hovering in the minds of economic planners. It was Pt. Jawahar Lal Nehru, the first Prime Minister of India, who broke away from the bondage of such dogma. He came out with a clear departure from these ideologies and advocated the application of modern science and technology in the development of the country. Large scale industries were established in Public (Governmental) and the Private Sector. A new wave of fast economic progress overtook the country.

The concept of small scale industry came up to replace the concept of village industries. They thrived well for some decades. When globalisation came to be accepted by India under the compulsion of the World Trade Organization (WTO), the small scale industry found itself difficult to survive. Goods from all over the world started reaching different corners of the globe. In these conditions, it was a fruitless effort to try setting up even large scale industries, let alone the small scale and the village industries. The present situation is, thus, totally different from the time, when the great Mahatma lived and preached the concept of independent villages and cottage-industries.

With the change in Indian conditions, it is time to respectfully depart from the Great Gandhian ideal of rural economy. It should now be boldly declared that the villagers will no longer be given sermons on producing their needs in their own villages or to shun the industrially

3

produced goods. It is time, to bring them in the mainstream of economic activity. While the villagers produce the vitally needed food grains and industrial raw material agriculturally, they should become consumers of the industrially produced goods. By this process, they will get the same advantages and improvement in their standard of living which the urban population has been enjoying for decades. The rural-urban divide has to be done away with.

We often hear reports in the media, of the protests of our leaders against the SUBSIDIES given by advanced countries to their farmers. Agriculture is, in fact, a dicey activity, the product of which comes after a long waiting period. It appears, people are not enthused to take up cultivation if they have alternative ways of earning their livelihood. In the U.S., for instance, only 2 per cent of the population is engaged in agriculture. That too, when huge subsidies are made available to them. Farming is still considered a retrograde type of occupation. A large number of jokes portraying the farmer of USA in an uncomplimentary way like the one quote given below:

A farmer married a lady hailing from a town and rode back to his ranch with his newly-wed bride on the horseback. When the horse stumbled, the farmer shouted, "That's once". When the horse stumbled for the second time, he shouted, "That's twice". When the horse stumbled for the third time, he jumped off and shot the horse dead. The newly-wed bride, badly shaken up by the incident, cried "YOU BRUTE!" To this, the farmer glumly replied, "Now, that's once".

In our own country, we are seeing that able bodied intelligent and enterprising people migrate to the urban area from their rural setting at the first opportunity. They want to escape the drudgery of a rustic occupation, agriculture, which is full of uncertainties and seek their future in the advanced urban sector. Such migration is not confined to the active and ambitious young people only. A large number of poor and destitute families also take to this course and come to towns and cities in search of livelihood. They contribute to the formation of shanty slums of the cities.

Dr. Abdul Kalam has been preaching in his capacity as the President of India for the creation of urban city-like facilities in the villages, so that such socially disturbing process of migration could be stopped.

There are two aspects of such improvement of the villages as has been proposed by Dr. Abdul Kalam. One is the improvement of the infrastructure of the village. Construction of link roads to the villages as well as the roads of the interior of the village comes as the first priority in the scheme of things. Next comes the improvement in the sanitation of the village. Electricity and, if possible, supply of running water comes next. The third priority would be to improve the housing. Providing health care and medical facilities will come as an immediate next requirement. Further on, community centers, administrative buildings like Panchayat Ghar also come in the list of such planned village upliftment.

On the other hand, the theory being propounded in this book is a little different from what has been stated above. What has been described above is in short the up-gradation of the public utilities and general facilities of the village. This programme does not touch directly the daily life of the villager, nor does it enthuse the residents of the village to come forward and share in these developmental works.

It may be recalled that the Community Development Programmes launched immediately after the Independence failed to catch the fancy of the rural masses. One of the major reasons for this, according to the author, is that there is a lack of an organisation which may be called "Community" in most of the villages. The exceptions are to be found in the tribal villages. In the non-tribal areas the village comprises individual households. They are grouped according to the religious and caste classification. The centuries-old division of the village society cannot be wished away easily. The deprived sections in the village society comprising the scheduled caste continue to simmer under the oppressive social and religious disabilities. Beginning with the abolition of the practice of Untouchability by the Constitution of India in the year 1950, efforts have been made to do away with such an inhuman and shameful thinking and practice in the society. The evil has persisted.

Let alone these low and miserable communities, even a higher and more affluent part of the society is also divided on caste lines. People refer to their neighbours and acquaintances by their caste denomination. The oft-repeated elections have sharpened the caste based divide of the village. Political leaders thrive on exploiting the set proclivities of the rural masses. Elections are won or lost on the basis of the caste-wise voting. Thus, instead of leveling down the caste and community barriers, the elections have helped only to make them more and more sharply divided.

From what has been stated above, it would be seen that there is no coherent village unit which may be called the "village community". The reason for the failure of the Community Development Programs was, according to the author largely due to this inherent factor.

Then the question is, how to tackle the centuries old problem demit poverty and absence of enterprise. The answer appears to be, that the village households should be reached directly, with a plan for their individual improvement. Poverty, in its basic connotation, is the poverty of consumption. All attempts need to be directed towards, making the villager a good consumer. Food, shelter and clothing are the fundamental requirements for their survival. This ensures that the body and the soul of the villager, remains intact. In order to make him an efficient worker, capable of generating wealth, it is necessary that his daily needs, are understood after a thorough survey. The industrial society, now primarily serving the urban masses should divert a part of its production to meet these needs, as far as possible.

Food security of the villagers is, of course, a primary requirement for an efficient management of Governance. Well fed children alone can grow into intelligent and capable adults. Extension of the Public Distribution System (PDS), is the surest way of ensuring this. It must be recognised that men cannot live by bread alone. They need a lot more things, to make their life safe, comfortable and then capable of energetic activity. The advancement in technology, has generated a latent urge, to possess and use modern facilities, devices and gadgets.

The Indian industries are now turning out a vast range of products, which are of direct utility, in the daily life of citizens. The urban society is avidly adopting these items. The rural society, on the other hand, is still denied the benefit of consuming or availing of these products. A visit to any common village, a little away from the urban markets, will bring out the fact, that people are living there

7

in a pre-Industrial era. Those, however, left out of such benefits, are helplessly watching, the trickling in of the benefits, of modern life in the rural area.

What is necessary at this stage, is to produce those items, in industries, which fit in with the life style of a poor villager. The concept of a self-sufficient village, in which people live of the resources of the village, must be banished. Simultaneously, there should be a movement for the rural orientation, of a large number of industries, producing utility goods.

The rural masses of India frankly speaking, are a drag on the progress of the whole country. Unless the 70 per cent of the total population of our country living in rural India, marches side by side, with the rest of the urban population, our clamor of rapid progress, will prove to be hollow claim. Any observer of the international scene, will not fail to assess the economic condition of the country, by reference to the vast number of poverty ridden people of the villages.

What did the industrial revolution achieve? This revolution introduced the techniques of mass production of goods. A large number of utility products, came into the market and became available ever to the ordinary members of the society, at a reasonable price. Earlier, most of these products used to be produced by craftsmen, by their individual skill and labour. They were hardly ever available, on a mass scale. A large number of weaker sections of society, were denied the use of many essential items, which are readily available in plenty today.

In India, the industries targeted their products for the affluent sections of the society. Production was, quite naturally, dictated by the profit motive. The benefits of Indian industrial revolution, therefore, stopped short at the doors of the urban society. It is true, that big landlords of the rural area, did avail of such items and thus became the envy of the large number of poor villagers, living in their vicinity. There was no attempt to produce such special goods which would fit in, with the purchasing power of the ordinary villagers. In India, the industrial revolution, in whatever magnitude it came, served only to deepen the urban-rural divide. The net result has been, that nearly half of the Indian population, has not reaped the benefits of the change, brought about by the great Industrial revolution.

What is most lamentable is the fact, that even after half a century of the independence of the country, the rural scene in general, remains as pitiable as it was earlier. The industrial policies, never bothered to turn the direction of the industries, towards the villages. The sacred idea, of keeping the rural people dependent on the products of the village industries, perhaps, gave a pretext to keep the rural masses out of the reach of industrial products. At the same time, they kept the urban society with plenty of availability of these products.

It was believed that products of the village carpenters, blacksmiths, weavers, cobblers and such other artisans, will generate employment and will become a source of earning a livelihood, for a section of the village population. In practical terms, this theory translated itself into a situation where these artisans had to depend on the purchase of their products by the cultivators living in the villages. The agriculturist was, and is, himself a poverty-ridden person. He suffers from the vagaries of the season, failure or excess of rains or hail-storms, coming at the time when the crop is ripe and ready to be harvested. What economic support, could such poor buyers give to the village craftsmen, can be well imagined. The two, the cultivator and the artisan, make a mutually impoverishing combination. The rural economy ought to be allowed to develop, unfettered by previous theories and dogmas. The village society should not be treated anymore as guinea pig for experimentation of economic theories.

◻◻◻

2

High Expectations and Poor Support System

Successive governments, headed by different political parties at the Centre and at the States, have come and gone, leaving the rural economy where it was a 100 years ago or even before. The contribution of the rural sector in a highly developed figure of G.D.P., has touched the highest watermark of around 20 per cent. When the growth rate of G.D.P. has been nearly 9 per cent, the share of the rural agricultural sector, has been limited to a maximum of 2 per cent or 2.5 per cent.

The backbone of Indian economy has been the production of agriculture products. The authorities running the economic affairs of the country, have been satisfied by ensuring "Food Security" in the country. This has led to a thinking that production of about 200 to 250 million tonnes of food grains per annum, is all that is required to be contributed by the rural agricultural sector. Tall orders are estimated from those in authority, demanding a steady improvement in the production of food crops. It was expressed by the Prime Minister in 2007, that 30 million tonnes of pulses, 70 million tonnes of wheat and 100 million tonnes of paddy or rice are required to be produced by the farmers, in order to raise the growth rate of the agricultural sector to 4 per cent, out of the total growth of 9 per cent. The only indication of the methodology of achieving this goal, was that more credit would be made available to the agricultural sector. A measure of consideration or mercy shown to this sector, was only to say that the rate of interest on these loans would be kept low. There was no mention of any steps by which, the production efficiency and the living standards of the agriculturists, will be enhanced.

To be a strong and healthy worker, one needs good nutrition and good living conditions. An impoverished farm worker is unable to put in hard labour, required for producing a bumper crop. The agriculture sector is at present manned by people, having a low consumption level and corresponding low efficiency. All efforts of exhorting the farmer, to produce more will not have the desired result. The need of the farm sector is to strengthen the man behind the plough.

This has to begin from the childhood of the Farm men. If proper nutritious food is not available in sufficient quantity to the child, his physical and mental growth becomes stilted. The child needs protection, against diseases, like Pneumonia, Diarrhoea, Rickets and other primary complexes. These are highly debilitating diseases. Such diseased children cannot grow into hardy, sturdy and adults of robust health. Deficiency of iodine too results in mental feebleness. Protection against infectious diseases, like polio, typhoid, measles etc., should be done by giving doses of preventive inoculations. Adequate quantity of proteins and vitamins, can ensure that the child will grow into a physically and mentally fit adult. It has now been realised that investment in child health programmes, will yield very rich dividend. Building up of a healthy and strong rural society should begin from rearing healthy children.

Next to health care, is the need for proper pre-primary and primary education. Till a few decades ago, two out of every ten children, were either not going to school at all or were dropping out very soon from their studies. The village primary school is the prime factory, from where mentally alert, positively oriented and knowledgeable citizens originate and form the basic fabric of the society. Against our laudable success in the industrial field, there is a colossal failure in developing the human resources. The primary schools were left in the persons, of callously negligent hands where the dream of free compulsory primary education was totally lost sight of. The village schoolmaster, described in highly romantic terms by Oliver Gold Smith who built up England of the past centuries is nowhere to be seen in the post independence Indian rural scenario. The widespread mediocrity of the rural area, is the crop that we are now reaping, as a result of this criminal neglect.

Our rural schools, lag behind in suitable buildings, teaching material and above all, in committed well oriented teaching staff. In the absence of suitable residential accommodation, the school teachers prefer to stay in the neighbouring towns and pay a casual visit to the school. They would come late, and go away early. There is rampant absenteeism, due to the headmasters lack of authority, to control their truant teachers, being themselves guilty of the same default, as of their juniors.

A famous Public Administration expert Paul Appleby, who was invited to India to advise on the subject, had commented that nothing gets done in India, unless it is inspected. This could not be more true and applicable in any field than in the field of rural primary education. During the colonial rule, the schools inspections were conducted with utmost regularity and strictness, as a result of which, the product of the primary schools was of a high quality. Today if we find a fast deterioration in social and personal behaviour, a ting of lawlessness and absence of moral values, the neglect of our primary education, is to be blamed for these.

In place of the Government run institutions, private primary schools have mushroomed in the urban area. They charge exorbitant admission and tuition fees, in return for high-grade education. This system has created a dichotomy in the society, the rural educated man, growing up as an inferior citizen. Urban parents of even modest means, have been satisfied with seeing their children doing fairly well in these schools. The rural schools have been consigned to the neglect of the society.

STRENGTHENING THE RURAL MANPOWER

As has been discussed earlier, the improvement in the quality of manpower in the rural area has to begin from rearing healthy children. Only healthy children will grow into robust adults, capable of putting in hard labour, needed for taking forward the rural society. The health care of the entire rural masses, is a challenging task for the developing nations like India. If the children's health problems are taken care of, the adult population will enjoy reasonably good health.

Besides health, the efficiency of the working population of villages requires support in respect of comforts. Given a good measure of such facilities, the productivity of the workers will go up by leaps and bounds. Some of these items, leading to a qualitative change in the living standards, are given thereafter.

Improving Housing: It is nearly impossible to build new houses for villagers. What can be done is to add to and bring about improvement in them.

Ventilation and Lighting: Majority of the houses in the rural areas are built of mud walls and tiled roofs. The height of the sloping roof goes down very low at the end of the slope because the roof rests on walls of low height. The dwellers of these houses find these dark and dingy portions of the house, utterly ill ventilated and poorly lit, even during the daytime. A solution for these problems can be found, if small ventilators, iron bars or strong wire mesh are embedded in the mud walls. A steel or iron lid should be fitted in hung at the top in such a way that lid can be closed as and when, required by operating from inside the house.

Cemented Area for Kitchen and Bathing Place: The cooking area of the house should be cemented, as well as the bathing place. If we set apart one bag of cement for every rural house, this can take care of tremendous improvement in the villages. The house owner can be advised to have two areas, of about one square meter each one as the cooking area and the other for bathing place of the house. Half a bag of cement, will be sufficient to cover each of these places. With a cemented kitchen, cooking will be far more hygienic than what it is, with its mud flooring. Similarly, the bathing place will be much more convenient to use, than what it is with a mud floor. Bath water falls on the mud floor, it throws up dirt and mud on the person, while he is taking his bath. In fact, the difference has to be experienced by undergoing the ordeal of taking a bath on a mud floor. With these two small inputs, the level of day-to-day comfort and standard of living, will be raised very significantly. If carried out systematically on a large scale, it will bring about a revolutionary change in the rural scenario. Every bag of cement so utilized will go a long way in up-lifting the standard of living of the poorest of the poor in our country. There should be no hesitation in embarking on such a step. Diverting cement from its use in building multi-storied complexes and malls may pinch the affluent section of the society, but will on the other hand, go to lay the foundation of an egalitarian society. There is no dearth of limestone in the country. Earmarked cement plants can be set up to produce cement branded as for "Rural Consumption only". Such cement factories should be extended all facility of tax reliefs, credit facilities and cheap concessional rail and road transport facilities to and from the cement plant. Like the Green and White Revolution, it is now time to bring about a Cement-revolution. People at the helm of affairs, have to be imbibed with the spirit of "Think Village". Such people alone can bring about these changes in the country, the type of which occurred, when railway network was created throughout the country or the canal system was laid out in the Punjab! **This is what is meant by "Making Goods for Villagers"**.

EXTENDING CREDIT IN AN INNOVATIVE WAY

It is important to add a word of caution about the system of rural credit. The poor marginal farmer, who constitutes the bulk of the agricultural-production-force, is an inefficient financial manager. The money, which comes in his hands as a loan to improve his agricultural activity may not go into that channel. He is hard pressed to meet several essential non-agricultural needs of his family. There is every chance that the loan given to him may be misused for meeting such commitments, like repayment of outstanding private loans, marriages of daughters and sons, keeping his dilapidated house in a proper state for survival and so on. There are innumerable cases, where the money in the hands of the poor farmer, is cornered by his relatives as sub-loans. His children sometimes insist on buying consumer durables. The farmer finds it very difficult to resist such pressures and demands.

In short, in almost all cases of the loan, out of money coming in the hands of a farmer, a substantial percentage goes out into non-agricultural channels. As a result, the improvement expected in the farming procedures and production, due to the loan given, hardly ever meets the expectations. The ideal situation of the credit advanced to the farmer, finding its way directly into the improvement of the farm, exists almost nowhere.

Advancing credit to the farmers has led to a lot of misery, when the question of repayment of the loan arises. The cultivator finds himself utterly helpless, when the loan taken by him does not give him extra production and thereby extra earning. The unfortunate cases of large-scale suicides by farmers are the result of such situations. Advancing credit to the farmer is, in short, no way of ameliorating their lot.

कर्ज से सस्ती किसान की जान
पखवाड़े में तीसरी मौत एक और ने जहर खाया
भास्कर न्यूज भोपाल

It would be seen from the above, that making the credit available in cash to the farmer, is no way of improving either agricultural production or the lot of the farmer. Burdening him with debts is a counter-productive measure. Right from the time when the cultivators were given loans in the shape of Takkavi or Grow More Food (GMF) loans, the agriculturist has been simmering under the mentality of being a debt-defaulter.

Whenever credit facility is given to the industrial sector, a cash flow statement is prepared and the repayment capabilities of the intending debtors are clearly taken into account. Despite these precautions, huge sums of money advanced as credit to industrial houses, have turned into bad debts. Putting money in the shape of loans in the hands of the helpless farmer who is dependent on the vagaries of nature subject to the hazards of drought, excessive rains and hail-storms, besides the fluctuating market conditions, is nothing short of a gamble. The solution to this problem, is to be sought in ingenious methods of coming to the succour of the agriculturist.

On the other hand, some institutions of doubtful credibility, like Kangal Banks, entice the farmer to deposit their hard earned money on the promise of attractive rate of interest. Such fly-by-night companies, have done incalculable damage to the simple and gullible farmers. All told, the farmer is a very poor financial manager, unable to plan his expenditure schedule. Surrounded by poverty and deprivation, he feels an irresistible urge to spend on his immediate and pressing needs. It is futile to expect that he will use the cash received by hand, as loan, in bringing-about improvement in his farm. As a consequence, his capacity of re-paying the loan becomes feeble. With more credit being given in cash, he goes on becoming more and more burdened with debt. When such farmers are pressed for re-payment of loans, they are driven to take the extreme step of taking their own lives. How dangerous and futile it is, to give cash in the hands of a poor farmer, has not been fully realised by our planners.

NEGLECT OF PRIMARY EDUCATION IN RURAL AREAS

Nearly 70 per cent of India's population lives in villages. The callous neglect of education at the primary level, especially in the rural areas, has brought into existence a vast population of poorly educated men and women. In fact, even if they belong to a privileged class, they are fortunate enough to have access to a primary school. Those who are deprived of even this basic need of human society like primary education, fall in the category of illiterates. These illiterate citizens, together with the poorly educated rural masses, constitute the bulk of our voters. Thanks to our deep-rooted democratic system, even this ill-equipped populace, has performed admirably well in elections.

Our education system is faced with a dilemma, of imparting higher education of excellence on one hand and of providing basic primary education to the vast number of rural poor on other hand. Neither of these two can be neglected. We seem to have favoured the expansion of higher education, in preference to the spread of primary education. Schemes like "SARVA SHIKSHA ABHIYAN" (Education for all), have come too late on the scene. Almost two generations substained rural population have gone by without the benefit of proper primary education during the last 60 years of our independence. Priority was given to the development of the natural resources of the country and thereby bringing about economic development. The task of human resource development, received low priority during this period. We were content with enshrining the concept of "free compulsory education for all" in the nebulous chapter of our Constitution, "Guiding Principles of State Policy", the human resources of the country have remained, by and large, underdeveloped.

Due to lack of proper education, amongst the general masses, vast majority of people who lived in villages, failed to contribute to Population Control. These people failed to catch up, with the idea of raising small families. Family Planning could have gone down smoothly and effectively, if education was available to the rural poor. With a controlled growth of population, we could have performed far better in the field of economic development.

❑❑❑

3   Treating Villagers as Producers only

India's GDP has agriculture production as its main content. As is well known, we produced just about fifty million tonnes of food-grains at the time of our independence. There were periods of dire food scarcity in the decades immediately following our independence. The first Five-Year Plan was devoted to the development of agriculture. Gigantic River Valley Projects like Bhakhara-Nangal were planned and executed with a sense of urgency. Generation of electric power was linked with these projects. The Indira Gandhi Canal Project took waters of Bhakhara-Nangal to Rajasthan and converted this State from a desert to a lush-green fertile area. Flood Control was also one of the objectives of these schemes. The Hirakud Project of Orissa served the dual purpose of power generation and flood control besides providing irrigation to agriculture. Pt. Jawaharlal Nehru whose ceaseless efforts brought into existence such mega projects described them as the modern day centres of pilgrimage.

Despite these steps, agriculture did not take-off in any serious manner. Vast areas under cultivation continued to depend on the dicey rainfall. The demand for food grains escalated due to fast increase in population. Adequate health care leading to increase in longevity and life expectancy, combined with high birth rate contributed to the population-explosion. Some of us still remember the era, when the then Prime Minister, Lal Bahadur Shashtri gave a call for observing a weekly half day fast. A lucky break came to us when Shri C. Subramaniam, the then Agriculture Minister, happened to visit Mexico and brought samples of dwarf varieties of wheat and rice. With extraordinary ingenuity, Prof. M.S. Swaminathan of ICAR helped by Dr. Narman Borlaug of U.S. multiplied the seeds and brought about the Green Revolution, thereafter our annual food production shot-up, finally to 200 million tonnes- plus per annum.

It is gratifying to note that the availability of food grains to the people of our country became quite satisfactory. Huge stocks of food grains were stored in the godowns of the Food Corporation of India (FCI). The concept of "Food Security" was established. But the Public Distribution System (PDS) seemed to have lost its sheen because of easy availability of food grains in the open market.

With increase in food production, the prices of food-grains started falling, with the result that Government had to come forward with the policy of offering Support Price to the cultivator. A large scale procurement drive was undertaken, to assure the agriculturists of a reasonable return for their produce.

Some areas of the country like the three districts Kalahandi, Bolangir and Koraput of Orissa reported cases of utter poverty leading to even starvation deaths. The **Supreme Court of India** called upon the Collector of one of these districts, to report as to what measures were being taken to face this stark situation. Barring these few areas of endemic food scarcity, rest of the country enjoys a good measure of food security. It would be appropriate to evaluate the effect of Green Revolution on the general condition of the farmers.

A million dollar question is how does a farmer fare in this state of affluence brought about by the Green Revolution? First and foremost, the Green Revolution variety of seeds, required a lot of costly inputs. Five to six rounds of irrigations are required to sustain the crop of wheat. Fertilisers and Pesticides are essential to ensure a good yield.

Only rich farmers who were in a position to afford these essential inputs could hope to get a bumper crop. Small farmers owning just about two hectares of land could not reap much benefit from the high yielding varieties of seeds.

Even these small farmers tried to derive some benefits from the high yielding qualities of the new seeds and resorted to borewells for irrigating their holdings. The shortage of power-supply to these tube-wells became a serious limiting factor. Three phase electricity supply was made available at odd hours only for a short duration. All in all, the real benefits of Green Revolution went to big and rich farmers.

The first Five Year Plan contains a very pithy statement that agriculture in India is just a way of life. People of the rural areas are engaged in agriculture, generation after generation, as a matter of compulsive engagement. The absence of any alternate employment or activity, forces them to stick to their traditional occupation. The nation has come to regard the farmer as a community engaged in feeding the entire population through their toil.

In the above viewpoint, the pleasures and pains of a farmer's life, are of little concern to the consumers of his products. The Agriculture Commission of 1929 for the first time dealt with the problems of agriculture of the country. The focus, however, was not on the farmer but on his activity of agriculture. Only recently, a Commission on the conditions of farmer had been constituted under the Chairmanship of Dr. Swaminathan. **This Commission has made an attempt to look into the problems of the farmer rather than the problems of his occupation, i.e. agriculture.** The agriculturist, as well as the landless labourers dependent on him, are expected to solve their deep rooted problem of poverty on their own. As long as a sumptuous crop reaches the market and food grains are available at a reasonable price, it is presumed that all is well on the agricultural front!

EXTENDING LOANS TO FARMERS (IS IT THE SOLE PANACEA FOR RURAL PROBLEMS?)

Right from colonial days, granting loans to the farmers has been treated as the sole method of providing succour to the farmer. Originally Cooperative Credit Societies provided loans. Government also gave loans directly in the shape of Taccavi loans. After the Banks were nationalised, the task of extending loans to farmers was entrusted to these Banks. A large number of branches of these Banks were established in the rural areas. Loan-Melas were organised on a large scale and handsome credit was extended to the agriculturists in a very liberal manner. Main activities for which those credits were extended was digging of wells and tube-wells, levelling of fields, making bundings around the fields, purchase of bullocks and later on tractors.

Effect of Granting Loan to Farmers

The Block Development Officers encouraged people to avail of the credit facility and improve their farming

24

methods. The security for these loans was the mortgage of land belonging to the farmer. When incidents like failure of finding water in a dug-well or in a tube-well occurred, the cultivator was placed in an unenviable position. On one hand, he failed to derive any benefit from the loan and on the other hand, the payment of instalments of loans became a burden. **In many cases, Recovery Certificates were issued to the Tahsildars for the realisation of loan by a coercive process like selling of the land**. When such instances came to light, the villager who was already under apprehension of the adverse official activities, became so scared that availing of credit facilities became unpopular.

Over the years, great emphasis was laid on inducing the agriculturists to accept loans. The performance of Bank Managers was judged by their ability to extend such loans. The process of actively granting loans resulted in more and more farmers becoming indebted to the banks.

In areas like the Vidarbha region of Maharashtra and in some parts of Andhra Pradesh, a new variety of cotton was introduced. Known as the BT Cotton, this variety used to yield better quality cotton fibre with a bumper yield. It had, however, two-drawbacks. Firstly, it needed irrigation facilities, secondly and more importantly, its seeds were not fit for sowing for the next crops. In the case of previously used varieties, the farmers used to store the seeds of the previous crop for sowing the next crop. With the new variety however, they had to buy new seeds for every season. Most of them took loans to purchase the new seeds. Since the yield was not up to the expected mark, due to lack of irrigation facilities, the burden of loan increased.

Banks took strict steps to recover their loans. Further, the private money lenders resorted to crude and oppressive methods for recovery of these loans. Under the pressure of such forceful recovery, the highly self-respecting cotton cultivators of Vidarbha, took to suicides. On average, as many as five suicides were reported from the districts of Vidarbha every week.

The Prime Minister of India took notice of this tragic situation and paid a visit to this region. He announced a relief package for the highly suffering population of this area. It was, however, a matter of great regret that the relief announced by the Prime Minister did not reach the poor farmers at all and suicides continued unabated. The only hope for the people of Vidarbha region is resting now on the promised loan relief package of Rs. 75,000 crores announced on All India basis package.

THIS BRINGS TO FORE THE QUESTION, WHETHER IT IS A PANACEA OR POISON TO EXTEND CASH LOANS TO FARMERS?

For a country like India, the economic base of which is agriculture and where as much as 70% of the population is dependent on it, progress in a real sense is possible only when this sector of economy develops. It has to grow by leaps and bounds. Inputs for bringing about this change have been mentioned below.

NEGLECT OF INPUTS REQUIRED FOR AGRICUL-TURAL PRODUCTION

Irrigation

Water is the most essential ingredient for improving the condition of the farmers. Taking water of irrigation to the parched agricultural lands, is the first and foremost requirement for uplifting the total economy. Nearly 70% of the population of India directly or indirectly depends on agriculture. Their prime need is irrigation. Merely upgrading urban commerce and industry will never give a facelift to India. It must, therefore, be realized that any expenditure, howsoever large it may be, ought to be willingly incurred for strengthening the very roots of our economic system. Let us not indulge in the illogical method of sprinkling water on the leaves and flowers of plants while neglecting to provide water to the roots.

The standard and time-honoured system of large scale irrigation, is the creation of large dams across the rivers which take water to the fields by flow irrigation through canals. This has worked wonders in Punjab. Recently, there has been a strong opposition to the creation of such dams because of the submergence of land under the dam-water. As an alternative, bore wells have come up as an effective substitute for flow irrigation by canals. The bottle-neck in this system is the shortage of electricity. If we can produce more power by thermal or nuclear sources, lift irrigation by tube wells will pick up very fast. Recharging of underground water should be undertaken by impounding rain water in stop-dams of rivulets and also by construction of small tanks of 2 to 4 acres in the midst of the cultivated lands. There are a few very interesting projects coming up to better the irrigation of our country which when completed will yield good results in the field of agriculture.

Power

The power requirement of agricultural sector has not been taken into account while planning power generation.

27

Manufacturing sector claims the highest priority. Domestic consumption comes next. The requirement of farmers for energising the lift irrigation usually comes at a low priority. Electricity is diverted to the farms at odd hours of the night, when the demand in the other sectors goes down. It is hoped that someday dedicated power generation exclusively created to meet the need of the farm sector will be setup all over the country. If nuclear power generation comes into vogue in our country, we should allow the farm sector to take highest priority in availing of this power.

Seeds and Fertilisers

There is a constant shortage of seeds and fertilisers in the rural areas. This has led to black marketing of these items. Instances have been reported of looting of trucks carrying fertilisers. The solution lies in setting up more seed multiplication farms and more fertiliser factories all over the country.

Insecticides

The high yielding crops require effective plant protection. The gas tragedy of Union Carbide Bhopal gave a setback to the production of the standard insecticide called "Savin". Other chemical factories have now come up to fill the gap.

AGRICULTURAL MACHINERY

The traditional plough drawn by bullocks has been replaced by farm tractors all over the country. Branches of various banks setup in rural and semi-rural areas have been extending credit facility for the purchase of tractors. These tractors are being hired by the neighbouring small farmers on hourly basis. The Central Agricultural Engineering institute located at Bhopal works on animal drawn and power driven agricultural machinery. Its product have been given to commercial firms for mass production. It appears there is a long way to go before such efficient machines become readily available to farmers all over the country. This core sector of industrial production needs to be developed with greater vigour.

One of the reasons why agriculture gets a step-motherly treatment in matters of development is that, Ministers, Senior Officials & Planners, who decide the fate of agriculture and the agriculturists, have a very negligible practical experience of undertaking cultivation. This situation is ordained to be so because a poor or even middle level agriculturist cannot ever aspire to become a senior official having a say in agricultural planning. On the other hand, it is not expected that a senior official connected with the planning of agriculture, will have his roots in agriculture, the two being mutually exclusive. It reminds one of the historical expectations that **"Philosophers will be the Kings"** (Philosophers do not possess the chicanery required to become a king and kings can ill afford to be philosophical). There is an appalling ignorance about agriculture. In fact about the rural life amongst city dwellers, few educated persons of urban areas know what is "kharif" and what is a "rabi" crop. (The crops sown in the rainy season like paddy are the Kharif crops and those sown in winter like wheat and gram are the Rabi crops.) They have little idea of what an acre and hectare is? As is well known that an acre is an area of land measuring 22 yards in width and 220 yards (a furlong) in length the total area of acre is thus 220 × 22 which is 4840 square yards or 43560 Sq feet. A hectare is on the other hand is a piece of land measuring 100 × 100 Metres i.e. 10000 Sq. meters. On a rough estimate, 2.5 acres make one hectare.

Governmental activity in India has a strong urban bias. The Urban population constituting about 30 per cent of the total population runs their own cycle of production, consumption and employment. The rural population engaged in agriculture is treated as a support agency commissioned to produce food grains and a few agricultural raw materials (like cotton) for their use.

❑❑❑

4 Agriculture—Just a Way of Life

The First Five Year Plan document contained a very appropriate description of Indian agriculture scenario. It is stated here that agriculture is just a way of life and not an industry in India. Those who are engaged in agriculture go through the routine of preparing the fields, sowing, harvesting and selling the produce after retaining their share for their consumption. Generation after generation, men and women of rural areas have been going through this routine. The profitability of agriculture has never been a matter of concern as several festivals all over India are connected with agricultural schedule and people go through the seasonal festivity aligned with agricultural operations.

The village people lead a highly static life. They occasionally go out for pilgrimage which gives them the only chance to travel beyond their surroundings. Added to this factor is the fact that a vast majority of village dwellers are born, grow up attain youth to become parents and ultimately become old in the same surroundings. Another factor of their social life is that there is intrusion in their privacy and family affairs by their neighbours. Thirdly, the village society also keeps a vigil on every household. Any aberration is frowned upon. The unwritten laws of the village community are enforced with a firm hand by the village elders, who usually belong to higher sections of the society.

One of the evil aspects of village life is the jealousy amongst people. There is so much of inter-personal rivalry in the community that any individual or family growing beyond the average level of achievement is subjected to unfair interference. It is intolerable for most of the households to see that their neighbours attain better standard of living. The solution of this problem has been found by more enterprising individuals in the shape of migration to urban areas. It is often a matter of adverse comment that in towns and cities, most people do not interact with their neighbours living next door. Everyone tries to protect his privacy and individuality. Friends and relatives are usually persons living at distant places and very few neighbours are close friends. This system has evolved due to the need of families or individuals to mind their own business and follow their own goals in life. The value of this self imposed isolation is generally not recognised. One has to see the dark side of close neighbourly relations in the village society. Any attempt to go beyond the norm is snipped at. It is difficult for the resident of an urban settlement to realise, what it means to spend your whole life in the good, bad or indifferent proximity of the same families and the same — neighbours. One of the reasons why there is stagnation in village society is that there is too much intermingling and the resultant leg pulling amongst neighbours.

One of the principles of classic management lay emphasis on "Group Norms". Workers in a modern establishment observe adherence to an unspoken group norm. None of the members of a group is allowed to avail of benefits beyond what is available to the rest of the group. On the other hand, none of the members appreciate if one exceeds the level of activity expected from the group. Neither lethargy nor over-activity is tolerated by the peers. This principle applies with vengeance to the village community. No wonder, people in the village have confined themselves to the norms and standards set by the village society. Those who have ambitions beyond this, have to migrate to the towns and cities. The contribution of this factor, jealousy, which promotes mass scale migration to urban areas has not been fully realised yet.

There is a Sanskrit verse in praise of the deity, Devi, which runs as follows:

Ya Devi sarvabhuteshu shraddha rupen sansthita,
Namastasyai Namastasyai Namastasyai Namonamah.

Salute to the divine spirit shraddha (devotion) i.e. reverence, which is installed (by nature) in the heart of every person.

Seeing the ways of the world, it appears equally appropriate to add one more verse as follows:

Ya Devi sarvabhuteshu eersha rupen sansthita,
Namastasyai Namastasyai Namastasyai Namonamah.

Salute to the divine spirit eersha i.e. jealousy, which is installed (by nature) in the heart of every person.

It is to be realised that jealousy plays an important role in encouraging people to make extra efforts to succeed in their goal. So long as this spirit is confined to accepting a challenge and trying to excel, it has positive value. When, however, this spirit deteriorates into a cut-throat competition in which the other competitors are pulled back maliciously, it becomes a negative factor in interpersonal relationships. The village society, somehow, suffers from this serious drawback. There is another concept in the classical Sanskrit literature. It is *Matsar*. It refers to a higher level of jealousy in which one does evil things to others without deriving any benefit to himself. Both *eersha* and *Matsar* are found among the village community in a fairly large measure. Instances are often noticed where the people of the village society go to the extent of causing harm to others even when they do not stand to gain by such action.

Gandhiji's emphasis on energising the village community was an important step in the right direction. When the independence movement left its urban base and turned to involve the rural people, it became a mass movement capable of shaking the British Raj from its roots. His idea of a self sufficient village, meeting its needs by its own products was a fanciful concept. This scheme of things pre-supposes the existence of a highly cooperative society in the village. It is presumed that the cultivators and the artisans of the village community will be collaborating to run the economy of the village. The cobbler will be happy to produce footwear, the man owning the oil seed crusher machine (kolhu) will be satisfied with his business of supplying oil to the village, and the carpenter will devote himself to making and mending the wooden implements used by the villagers and so on. This idealistic scenario of the rural community is actually far from reality. Human nature being what it is, the village is an assemblage of groups at logger-heads with each other. Education has not penetrated into the community thinking of the village. Going a step further, it can be stated that there is no cohesive and compact society in the villages.

The Community Development Programmes started soon after the Independence, failed to yield the expected results because there was no "Community" as such in existence, as envisaged by the planners of these programmes.

It may be recalled that the first developmental activity undertaken in late forties was in the shape of Development Blocks. They were funded by the Ford Foundation of U.S.A and generated a great deal of enthusiasm. The Minister for Development, Mr. S.K. Dey became a pivotal figure in India for some time. Though motor vehicles were a rarity in those days, all the Block Development Officers were provided with a jeep. Assistants to deal with subjects of Agriculture, Social welfare, Education, Co-operatives etc. were posted in each and every development block to assist the BDOs, who were selected from senior level gazetted officers. They were trained in celebrated training centres at Nilokheri and Baxi Ka Talaab.

As the influence of Socialism overtook our country and the balance of our friendship tilted in favor of USSR against the USA, Minister S.K. Dey and his development blocks faded into insignificance. So far, the developmental machinery was a separate entity from the Revenue and General Administration. A few years later, the administrative setup was to be given the responsibility of handling development work.

Supply of Jeeps to BDOs. had caused a lot of heart burning amongst their counterparts, the Sub-Divisional Magistrates and Tehsildars. The thinking in the Central and State Governments, (dominated almost in the entire country by the Congress party) turned lukewarm towards the Ford Foundation funded developmental machinery. In one of the states, Madhya Pradesh, even the post of the Development Commissioner who was heading the developmental machinery was abolished by the then C.M.

of the Congress Party, Pt. D.P. Mishra. Similarly the post of BDO was also played with. It was sometimes upgraded or downgraded and at times even abolished.

The fervour created in the early years of independence, of bringing about rural development, faded out over the years. As stated above, the normal administrative setup of the districts, was assigned the task of development, alongside its normal duties. This continued for several decades.

Then came the era of Village Governments. The Constitution of India, was amended to give constitutional recognition to the local administrative bodies, like the City Corporations, Municipalities and Village Panchayats. Emphasis was laid on grass root planning. The institution of District Development Councils, was empowered, to undertake developmental activities in the district, in accordance with their own plans.

The Role of Elections in Shaping the Village Community

Even though elections had been taking place every five years, for the Central and State Governments, there was no statutory provision for elections at the Village Panchayat level. This was brought into vogue by the constitutional amendment.

Elections have a tendency to divide people into groups and factions. When this happens on a large scale, as a result of the elections, to the Central and States Legislative bodies, the evil of dividing the people into separate factions, does not create much problem. This evil has, however, created havoc in the rural setting. The small village community got torn into factions. Those who won the elections, looked down upon those people who did not support them at the hustings, as more than their opponents, infact almost like enemies.

Elections in a democratic system have the beneficial quality, of allowing the view of the majority to prevail. At the same time, it leaves the defeated minority, with a sense of frustration. In any case, the election process leaves behind a schism in the village population. The absence of the sense of belonging to a community is further smashed by the inevitable activity of elections.

No substitute for the process of elections, has so far been found in the civilized society. This must, therefore, be accepted, as the price to be paid, for the practice of democracy on all levels.

Local Planning

After the local centers of administration came into existence, as constitutionally recognized entities, there came into being, a new trend in planning, which more or less reversed the original emphasis, on the scheme of a centralized plan, as envisaged by Mahalnobis. The new thinking in this direction – was to start planning from grassroots. Decentralized planning, helped in development, by highlighting the local needs. It therefore, showed results, which appealed to the rural masses. Matters of immediate concern to the community, were thus taken care of. Enough funds were directly allocated to these local bodies from the Centre. The other side of this picture, is that due to dissention accompanying the divide caused by elections, the process of planning, has played into the hands of one faction or the other.

If one takes a wholistic view, no major developmental activity, could be expected to come from local planning. This cannot become a substitute for a centralized plan. Matters, like the construction of irrigation dams, thermal or hydro-electric power projects, laying out National Highways, setting up of fertilizer factories are examples of some such subjects, falling within the competence of a centralized plan.

Fortunately, the local planning has not totally substituted the concept of centralised planning.We are seeing the remarkable results of a centralized plan, in many areas. One such item is the creation of Bhakhara-Nangal multipurpose dam. It has yielded dramatic results. The Indira Gandhi Canal has turned Rajasthan from a barren desert into a fertile green orchard. While it was earlier receiving a scanty or even a negligible rainfall, it is now receiving its full measure of monsoon rains.

If we wish to change the fate of the farmer, we should lay emphasis on centralised planning. We need to take bold steps, to create more such gigantic projects and not get stuck up, in the quagmire of local planning. The interest of the huge rural population, which is dependent on agriculture, should be our prime concern.

In some areas, problems are being faced due to construction of dams. A few people are raising their heads in a revolting manner, especially those who are losing their agricultural land and property, due of submergence. Such people gang up together, under the rather misguided and dubious leadership of some self-serving leaders. The principle of the greatest good of the greatest numbers is totally lost sight of, for short term gains, which is the objective of such political enthusiasts. No doubt, such activists serve to highlight the problems of the displaced families, but they completely ignore the benefits accruing to a vast majority of persons and the whole nation, from such projects.

Compensation to such oustees ought to be given, as far as possible 'land for land'. Cash paid as compensation, disappears from the pockets of these people, without leaving them with any source of income, as an alternative to the land which they lost. The same situation is faced by these families, as is seen in the case of extending cash loans to farmers, as discussed earlier.

It is realised that availability of land to be offered as compensation, is limited. The project management should make an attempt to buy lands wherever available and offer them to the displaced families in spite of the high cost of such land.

❑❑❑

5   Treating Agriculturists as Bonded Labourers

The memory of the last few decades of 20th century takes one to the scenario of a grave situation on the food front. Till the green revolution initiated by the dwarf varieties of seeds brought from Mexico, by the then Union Minister of Agriculture, Mr. C. Subramaniam and further propagated by the efforts of the great agriculture scientist Prof. M.S. Swaminathan, there was a dismal picture of food shortage all over India. In those days, the cultivator was compelled to sell his product at a price dictated by the Government. The farmer had to deposit what was popularly known as "Levy" to the Revenue Officers. This came to be known as the "Procurement Drive". Although the entire produce was not taken away in this drive from the farmer, he always had the terror of the Procurement Officers in his mind.

It can be argued in favour of the then prevailing system that Procurement of the Levy was necessary to keep the Public Distribution System (PDS) functional. Supplying the entire population with ration on a equitable scale and at a reasonable price was the prime concern of administration at that time. The poor and the needy all over the country could be saved from food scarcity and even famine like conditions due to this effort.

There is, however, the other side of the picture also. The people subjected to such coercive procedure were agriculturists, who were made to pay for being in the agricultural sector of the country. Their storehouses and granaries were subjected to "raids" by the official agencies. There is a practice of storing grains by digging dry well-like pits underground for the storage of some types of grains. These storages, called "Bandas" used to be dug open to recover the Levy. There were cases where the cultivator was not able to produce the quantity expected from his agricultural holdings. As a result, such people are known to have actually bought food grains from the market and paid the Levy.

The agriculturist was thus made to part with his produce for a laudable cause. Now the question arises; do the agriculturists have a similar benefit of the procurement of the industrially produced items of their needs? Is any procurement drive started, for providing them with irrigation pumps, water pipes, agricultural implements and so on at administered prices and by imposing a Levy on the producers of such items? Do the cultivators get any benefit or relief corresponding to their suffering from procurement of levy from them? And this is done with a strong hand by officials of the "Procurement Drive". Any default in this respect could lead to humiliation of the farmer, who resist the coercive process of recovery of Levy beyond their capacity. They can do so only, at the peril of facing the wrath of the administrative machinery. Village level officers like Revenue Inspectors and Patwaris who hold a strict control over the cultivators, were employed for collecting the food grains of the agriculturists and they could ill-afford to annoy them, much less take up cudgels against them. Ensuring food security for the urban masses, who were the prime beneficiaries of rationing, under the Public Distribution System, may be a step in public interest but there is no *quid pro quo* to the farmer at whose cost this charity is done. In all fairness to the farmers, items of industrial production used by the cultivators should also be subjected to a similar Levy system. A portion of industrial products ought to be earmarked for sale in the rural areas.

The agriculturist of India suffers not only by shortage in production, caused by various natural factors like failure of monsoon or floods due to excessive rains, but he stands to suffer also, paradoxically, by excessive production! This works like this. There is a very delicate balance between the shortage and excess of the agricultural produce. It is true that production of less than the expected crop, turns his fortunes in the negative direction. On the other hand, when the climatic conditions are favourable, the cultivator is induced to invest, plenty of inputs in his crops. As a result, there is excess production. Here again, he faces a pitiable situation. Because the evils of excessive production start chasing him.

Supported by favourable climatic conditions, he is inclined to invest liberally in raising the more crop than in the normal years and incurs more expense. He pins his hopes on getting a bumper harvest. When, however, he takes his produce to the grain market (Mandi), his frustration knows no bounds. The cartels of grain merchants (aadhatia or Dalals or brokers), offer him unremunerative prices, claiming that the excessive production has brought down the price level. It is not uncommon to find that the grain merchants gang together and force the cultivator to sell his produce at the dictated low price. Having once carried his harvested materials to the nearby market, he is in no position to bring back the produce to his village, as the facility of safe storage of agriculture produce is sadly missing in most of the villages and also because he is unable to incur expenses in bringing back it to the village.

In addition to this, Government have often intervened to resort to monopoly buying of agricultural products, directly or indirectly, especially the cash crops like cotton. In some states, bales of cotton are directly purchased by a governmental agency. The payment of price, on the basis the receipt issued by weighment agency of the mandi is made in a slow manner. In the case of sugarcane, "Societies" have been created who buy sugarcane by putting the cultivators in a compulsive situation. Such cultivators cannot find buyers other than these societies. Here again, the actual payment of price takes weeks and months. The cheques issued to the farmers take a lot of time to be encashed. Fortunately, some reforms in agricultural marketing are being gradually introduced through Mandi Acts of the States.

The message of the low price calamity travels very fast back to the fields. Those cultivators, who are still busy in the final stage of their harvest, lose heart and stop giving finishing touch to harvesting. Those who have sown cash crops, like potato or onion, do not proceed further to dig out their produce from the field. Sugarcane & soyabean growers are known to have consigned their produce to fire in face of low returns in the market for these items. Some agriculturists, allow their cattle to graze in their fields instead of selling their produce at a unremunerative prices. Indian agriculture is subject to double jeopardy. Shortage in production obviously brings calamity but the travails and tribulations caused to the cultivator, by excessive production are generally not very apparent.

Suggestions to Overcome the Problem of Excessive Production

The solution to this problem can be found in establishment of a large number of warehouses in the midst of the cultivated lands. The State Warehousing Corporations were set up in most of the States to provide relief to farmers affected by drop in prices. These Corporations, set up almost half a century ago, acted by storing the agricultural products in a scientific manner and about 60 per cent of the prevailing market price was paid to the cultivator. This payment was made in such a systematic manner that there was no scope for any bungling with the innocent poor farmers. The Corporation only issued a receipt for the grain deposited. The payment of cash, was done by a Bank on the basis of this receipt. The gradation of the quality of items deposited did leave some scope for corrupt practices still their total effect was almost negligible. Having received sixty percent of the price, the cultivator could manage to meet his immediate needs. When the market improved, he could take back his deposited food grains from the warehouse and sell them in the market.

This system has, for reasons unknown, not picked up as it should have. If implemented with sincerity, it could bring several benefits to the farmer as well as to the consumer. Firstly, the preservation of food grains in a scientific manner can prevent the huge loss suffered due to the menace of rats and insects. Further, the cultivator will not be compelled to sell his produce at unprofitable rates. At the same time, he will be in a position to meet his urgent needs by receiving about sixty per cent of the price of his produce. This will save him from dependence on the much-maligned village moneylenders. The tragic cases of suicides by farmers, due to their inability to repay the loans of the moneylenders, can altogether disappear.

While this will be of use for the more stable food grain crops, there is also need for cold-storages to preserve the perishable items like potatoes, onions and fruits. There is a heavy consumption of electricity in running these cold storages. If we can ensure a steady and dependable supply of electricity (which may be possible after the nuclear power projects become a reality), the entire rural, agriculture oriented, country side should be dotted with such cold storages.

The profitability of cold storages can be judged by the fact that items like potatoes are stored immediately after the coming of the crop, at the rate of about Rs. 2 per kg. When this item is taken out for sale, after about six to eight months, the price of potato rises to about Rs. 10 per kg.

Fruits and vegetables can become available to the consumers all the year round if we set up cold storages in large numbers. Private parties are quite interested in setting up these establishments if they are provided soft loans and assured electric supply. Government will do well to encourage this activity by taking care of the financial and power supply factors. More and more farmers are now taking to horticulture. Their produce can earn them a high profit, if their products duly preserved in cold storages, become available after the season of their production.

The above mentioned projects, the Warehousing Corporation and the cold storages, can uplift agriculture to a highly profitable venture. The eternal poverty which is the curse of agricultural sector, will change the face of the countryside from eternal poverty to eternal riches.

❏❏❏

6   Importance of Rural Areas in Overall Economy of India

Though our country is an agricultural country and huge population lives in rural areas, there is no mention of any rural events or activities in our print media.

There is a sharp divide between the rural and urban India. Such divisions exist in other countries of the world as well. Special circumstances of India (for that matter, of all agriculture based countries), are that the urban sector is more dominating than the rural base of the country's economy. Industrial sector based in the urban areas, do contribute to the total Gross National Product (GNP) but the agricultural sector provides the foundation on which the urban sector thrives. The rural agricultural activity sustains the urban sector by providing not only food for sustenance but also raw materials, like cotton sugar cane etc. to towns and cities. This may sound as stating the obvious. The point being emphasised here, is that this is a ONE WAY TRAFFIC.

How this is going to be achieved, is a difficult question to answer. Left to itself, the urban sector is quite sanguine with the present day system being in which the produce of this sector is avidly consumed in the urban areas. This provides a ready market for its products. They do not need to hanker after the villager whose paying capacity is obviously limited. With ready buyers and high pressure advertisements, the urban consumer lends so much support to the urban manufacturing industry that they are not much bothered about the rural consumer.

As stated above, the basic fabric of the country, is made of the rustic rural masses who have assumed political importance after the introduction of adult suffrage— **'one man one vote'**. Every election finds vote-seeking political aspirants running to the remote villages to woo the rural voter. This has in someway, enhanced the bargaining capacity of the villagers. Demand for roads, schools, hospitals, opening of administrative centers like Taluka as or Tehsil offices are being raised. All efforts are made to satisfy these demands by the political activists. A similar movement needs to be generated to ensure that villagers have access to the goods which go to improving their standard of living.

The market forces cannot be depended upon to bring about this revolution. It would be necessary to intervene by active diversion of rurally useful industrial goods to the villages. The system of imposing levy on agricultural produce has been discussed in the previous chapters. A similar system of levy on industrial goods for rural consumption is required to be introduced on the urban industrial sector.

A part of the industrial production, should be stamped as "For Rural Consumption Only". Differential rates of excise duty may be given for such products. Steps like the refund of Sales Tax, can encourage or, at least, compensate the producers, for the loss suffered by them, for selling in the rural markets. A measure of compulsion combined with attractive incentives will ultimately divert the industrial production to rural areas.

Years that Brought Sea-change in Indian Economy

It will be of interest to record here the process of change through which India underwent in the last decades of the 20th century. It all began with political turmoil caused by Mandal and Ayodhya agitations during the Prime Ministership of V.P. Singh, who suddenly announced his Government's acceptance of Mandal Commission recommendations to check-mate the political manoeuvres of his rival, Dy. Prime Minister Devi Lal. V.P. Singh wanted to project himself as the champion of Other Backward Classes (OBC). In this enthusiasm, his government conferred the award of Bharat Ratna on late Baba Saheb Ambedkar. This set the practice of giving this honour also to departed leaders like Subhash Chandra Bose. Many people, perhaps cynically, suggested that in keeping with this practice, this award could be given to great leaders of the past like Mahatma Gandhi, Guru Nanak Dev and even Lord Buddha.

In the same year, a great international crisis developed due to the invasion of Kuwait by Iraq. As a result, the price of oil soared sky high. Coupled with the political turmoil within the country, high oil prices caused havoc in the country. An unannounced rationing of Petrol and Diesel, by way of closing down the pumps at 6 p.m. on week days and 12 noon on Sundays, was introduced.

Further, as a part of promise in the poll manifesto, all loans of farmers were written-off. After issuing a historic waiver, government amended it to cover loans up to Rs. 10,000/- only. The borrowers have already stopped paying their loan instalments, in anticipation of the loan waiver. This gave a big jolt to the Banking Sector and worst affected were the Co-operative Banks.

After this, came the political crisis in form of opposition to the implementation of the Mandal Commission Report. Students, all over the country resorted to violent agitations, causing serious damage to railway property. Several students committed self-immolation. Almost simultaneously, BJP announced that it will take-out a nationwide 'Rath Yatra', from Somnath to Ayodhya. The BJP leader L.K. Advani led this 'Rath Yatra' triumphantly across the country and was arrested, when he was going to enter Bihar. After the fall of the Government of V.P. Singh, Chandrashekhar became the Prime Minister with the support of Congress from outside. Not only that, Chandrashekhar had hardly the strength of 20 MPs of the opposition party.

During this period, a multinational army under leadership of USA, launched air attacks on Iraq, to drive it out of Kuwait. Just before this, Indian workers employed in Kuwait and Iraq returned to India due to loss of their employment. The income from their remittances, was thus stopped. All these factors deepened the economic crisis in the country.

Multiple Elections

The general elections had been held in November 1989. Soon after this, as early as in March 1991, another general election was forced on the country because of the withdrawal of support by Congress to the Chandrashekhar Government. The country lost its most promising young leader, Rajeev Gandhi, who was just about to take over the Prime Ministership of the country, in a murderous attack by LTTE, in Sri Perambadur, Tamil Nadu.

After the refusal of Sonia Gandhi to take over the reins of the Congress Party, P.V. Narasimha Rao was brought out from his political retirement, to lead the party and became the leader of largest single party to form the government.

The Narasimha Rao Era

After taking over the leadership of the country as Prime Minister in June 1991, Narasimha Rao took stock of the prevailing dire economic situation. India was about to become a defaulter, in its international financial commitments. The foreign currency reserves of the country were sufficient for imports, for about three months only.

The first step which he took in the right direction, was to bring a non-political and professional economist to head the Finance Ministry. This was the beginning of the political career, of retired RBI Governor, Dr. Manmohan Singh, who ultimately took over as Prime Minister in 2004. He brought another professional economist and incidentally another Sikh, Mr. Montek Singh Ahluwalia, as Finance Secretary, giving this post to a non-IAS person. Both had worked in IMF in World Bank and had good relations with these Institutions. With their help, Narasimha Rao worked out an economic bail-out package, with the help of IMF and World Bank. As an immediate measure, gold lying with the Reserve Bank, was airlifted to London and pledged with the Bank of England, as a part of the economic revival package, negotiated with IMF and World Bank, Dr. Manmohan Singh set in motion, the process of economic liberalisation, in his maiden budget in July 1991.

This was opposed by BJP, the Communists and other opposition parties, declaring it as a sell-out. They went to the extent of declaring, that the country would again be subjugated by some foreign agency, like the East India Company. Although BJP under the leadership of Atal Bihari Vajpayee as Prime Minister, accelerated the process of liberalisation and privatisation further.

Today, India is one of the fastest growing economies in the world. Instead of East India Company coming here to take over the Indian business, the reverse is now true, with companies like Tata Motors, acquiring famous British brands like Land Rover and Jaguar. Laxmi Niwas Mittal is now, the richest person in UK. Many Indian companies have gone on a purchase and acquisition spree, mostly in Western Europe and USA.

There has been a general improvement in the consumption pattern of urban people. Even in the case of rural masses, many remarkable services have become available. One of them is opening of the communication channels, by way of telephones and more so by way of mobile phones. It is true that many items required for uplifting the hygiene and nutrition of the rural people, are still wanting; a trend has been set up towards the upgradation of living standards. India has been able to brave the consequences of global economic depression and has maintained a fairly high rate of growth of about 6–8 per cent per annum. The credit for all this must go to PV Narasimha Rao. It is, indeed, an irony of circumstances, that this leader has been ignored and forgotten by his Congress Party, perhaps because of the demolition of the Babri Masjid, during his premiership!

The Jealously-Guarded Urban Cycle of Production, Consumption and Employment

When the wind of industrialisation reached India from Europe, the urban settlements got the maximum benefit. In fact, industrialization did not touch the rural areas at all. People living in vast majority in the rural areas of the country continued to be engaged for centuries, in the age-old profession of agriculture. There was migration of workers from the rural to urban areas, to reap the benefits of industrialisation. Most of these people, however, came for low level basic jobs of a repetitive nature. Limited by lack of education and deprived of the facilities of training, these workers remained at the lowest rung of the urban ladder.

The sea-port towns of Mumbai, Kolkata & Chennai, were the favoured centres of Industrialization. It was perhaps, because of this reason the British entrepreneurs chose to be near the sea-shore. The growth of these centers of industry was phenomenal. Huge Industries came to be established in the adjacent areas. They were originally owned by British companies. This situation continued, till the country attained independence. After this, many of these high profile companies, got transferred to Indian business magnates. Interestingly, such companies retained their original nomenclature. Very few people got to know about the actual new ownership of these companies.

The above situation was seen to have happened in a big way with the tea companies of Assam & Bengal. It is to the credit of the new owners of the tea gardens that the production of tea greatly improved under the Indian Management. Indian business houses went on acquiring, garden after garden, with a small and modest beginning. One can assign credit for this to business acumen of the 'Marwadis' of Rajasthan. The tea auctions originally taking place at Kolkata, were partially shifted to Guwahati. The saga of the tea industry is a model of transfer of industry from British hands to Indian entrepreneurs. At the same time, it shows that the Indian industrialist is in no way inferior to his predecessor, the British businessmen, in running industries.

Another success story, is of the steel industry of India. This grew at 'Kali Maati' which came to be known as Jamshedpur. The foresight of the father of Industrialization, Sir Jamshedji Nasherwanji Tata an Indian, built up the steel plant of Tatanagar. It was the biggest steel plant in the old British Empire, the plants of Sheffield and Birmingham not excluded. Like Tatanagar, other centres of industrialisation grew around Ahmedabad, Kanpur, Bhilai, Rourkela, Durgapur, Bokaro Steel City, Bangalore and some other cities.

The above mentioned process of industrial development, brought into existence, wittingly or unwittingly, a cycle of production, consumption and employment.

The beneficiaries of all these three processes were the urban people. Production of industries was intended primarily for the urban people. Some leftovers of the production were, of course, sent to the rural areas. This was, however, not the target area of the industrial production. The urban people were the main consumers. The benefit of employment in industries also went in the share of the urban people. Thus, about 30 per cent of population enjoyed the benefits of the industrial revolution in the country, by way of production, consumption and employment. The rural masses were left out of this cycle. They were expected to produce food grains and some raw materials, like cotton, for the industrialised urban sector of Indian society.

By its very definition, industry is an establishment for mass production of goods. Expecting the cottage industries, to provide adequate supply of goods to the country, would be a mere utopian dream. In my way of thinking about this triangle, the rural people need to be involved in this process first as consumers.

With the increase of demand, the industrialisation will get a boost. Industrial units can then be setup in small towns. They will act as nodal points, to provide employment to the rural people, in the vicinity of their place of residence. The troubles and travails of living in large metropolitan cities, will, thus, be greatly reduced. The growth of urban slums, will also be reduced by adopting this system. A lot of thinking needs to be directed towards bringing into existence this kind of a dispersal of industrial production units in the vicinity of rural areas. Such establishments will become the Growth Centers for uplifting the surrounding rural areas. Roads, Electric lines, Water Supply and Housing, will grow due to the demand of these industries. Strong incentives will be needed to encourage this development. Tax rebates, liberal credit facilities, building of good schools and colleges for the children of the executives and workers will have to come up in due course. This scheme of urbanising the village has already been put in action in the State of Gujarat.

In the previous chapters, a case has been made out, for the setting up of industries, producing goods for the rural population. Here, it is being suggested that such industries **as well as those serving the urban section of society** should be established in the midst of the rural areas. There should be no more licensing of industries in the already overcrowded cities.

Once Industries come near the rural areas, the opportunities of employment will become available to the villagers. These villagers will then be drawn into the cycle of consumption, production and employment. The wind of industrial revolution, will then start blowing, over the vast neglected agrarian sectors of our country.

With fragmentation of land holdings and the gradual loss of the fertility of the soil, agriculture can no longer provide gainful employment in the villages. A rational mix of industries and agricultural activity, is the solution for meeting the unemployment or underemployment of the rural masses.

Devising a Marketing Strategy for Goods Produced Specifically for the Villagers

The sale of the goods produced for the consumption of villagers is done by normal marketing process at present. Traders dealing in retail business, should be involved in carrying these items along with others, to the rural areas. The margin of profit should be such, that the consumer and the supplier, both feel happy about the transaction.

Retail traders, however, find the urban market so lucrative that they have very little incentive to reach the rural consumer. The buyers are small in number. Carrying goods to the interior of the rural areas, involves extra cost and logistic problems. It is, therefore, necessary that there is a separate marketing mechanism to undertake the task of carrying such goods to the villagers. The sale outlets cannot be made available to all the villages. Retail stores will have to be established at some nodal points. Normally, these stores should be available at a distance of about 5–8 kms from each other.

A trading company, ITC, has set-up commercial centres for the sale of items of their utility to the villagers called Chaupal. Such retail outlets are proving very popular with the village community. In some such stores, farmers get a credit card, after the sale of their produce to ITC and they can make purchase of their choices using this card. This kind of agrocommercial activity, is the forerunner of the plan, which will bring prosperity to the rural people.

Rural markets, known as Mandis, are coming up at various places all over the country, where the produce of the agriculturist is put to auction. The bidders, normally from the urban areas make bulk purchases of agricultural commodities from these Mandis which are controlled by a central agency, known as "Mandi Board". It will be a great benefit to have these marketing points, not only for the sale of the agriculture produce but also for the supply of industrial goods to the villagers.

Ever since this system has come into existence in an organised way, the agriculturists have been saved from the clutches of the greedy and unscrupulous grain merchants. Taking advantage of the helplessness of the poor cultivators, these traders used to buy the agricultural commodities at a very low rate. The system of weighing the commodities, was often helpful only to the buyers and the price of the items purchased, used to be paid after some delay. In addition, these traders use to extend loans to the farmers (who were always in need of money) and get them committed to sell their produce to that particular trader. In the interiors of the backward areas of erstwhile Vindhya Pradesh (of which the Capital was Rewa), many of these traders, would visit different villages. They used to take two ponies with them on which they loaded the agriculture produce. The measures used by them for purchasing the commodities, were larger in size than the standard measures to the disadvantage of the poor sellers. Due to lack of transport facilities, the cultivators were placed at the mercy of such traders. With the implementation of the 'Pradhan Mantri Gram Sadak Yojna' and the introduction of the 'Mandi Board', the farmer is now in a position to expect an accurate weighment and fair price for his produce. The bungling in the measuring or weighing of his commodity, is now a matter of the past.

If such a well-organised system exists for collection of the rural produce for urban consumption, the reverse process of carrying the consumer goods, needed in the rural areas should also avail of the same efficient mechanism.

Things which may be Produced for Villagers Industrially

In deciding which items should be produced specifically for villagers, one has to take into account the needs of the villagers, their paying capacity, their ability to properly use and maintain the items and the effect of providing such goods and services, in enhancing the efficiency of these people. No exhaustive list of such goods can be made out, yet a broad based catalogue can be drafted. For general consideration, some of these items are listed below:

1. **Agricultural Implements of Improved Variety:** Research centers of agriculture engineering, have been devising and developing highly efficient machines and implements; their production is left in the hands of some governmental organisations, like the Agro-Industries Corporations of state governments. Some other items have been thrown open to private industry

also but their interest is primarily profit making. As a result, excellent items produced as a result of intensive research, are not readily available in the market. The simple rural cultivator, is thus deprived of the benefits of research and development of modern implements and machines. It would be a step in the right direction, if the products of these researches and developments are manufactured on a large scale, at strategically located industries in the public sector. The cultivator should have free excess to these items, in agro product shops. A beginning has to be made in the direction of opening such agro service stores, in a few selected places. Such stores, in fact, can meet a lot of the requirements of villagers. The "Kissan" credit cards issued to the farmers, are highly suitable for these transactions. If improved and efficient, implements and machinery, are readily available, the agriculture scene of the country can be radically changed for the better. Whenever, any credit facility is to be extended to the farmer, he should be supplied with such items instead of being given cash loans. It has been discussed in the earlier chapters that the ordinary farmer is a poor financial manager. The cash reaching his hands finds several ways of being mis-applied in non-productive expenditure. The villager in general and the farmers in particular, ought to be our focal point of developmental activity. In the spirit of "Unto This Last", we have to carry the farmer forward by our special efforts. Only when he raises his earnings and thereby, his living standard, the nation can claim to be prosperous.

2. **Plastic Sheets for Covering Roofs:** The leaky roofs of rural houses can be effectively protected against rains if

well designed plastic sheets are made available for these houses. Villagers do use such sheets but these sheets are not specifically designed for covering the roofs against the onslaught of the fury of Monsoon. Providing RCC roofs for these houses is a very distant dream. What can be done to keep the house dry in the rainy season, is to provide a product of our Petro-Chemical industry. The otherwise much maligned PLASTIC, can provide relief and a big measure of happiness, by being used as a covering over the roof of rural houses.

3. **Raincoats and Gumboots:** As a measure of safety and convenience, the cultivator working in muddy and slushy soil, needs the covering of his clothes by plastic raincoats. Those who have had the chance to visit the world famous Niagara Falls of the US, will recall how very thin plastic raincoats provided by the management of Niagara protect the visitors from the droplets and the mist generated by the Falls. The same type of covering can be produced for supply to the cultivators of India on a mass scale. Working with dry clothes, the cultivator will become a more efficient worker. Added to the raincoat is the idea of providing a pair of Gumboots on a mass scale, for protection of the farmer against mud slush and snake bite. Our thinking has, perhaps, been so oriented in respect of the village dwellers, that imagining a villager clad in a raincoat and wearing a pair of gumboots, is beyond our perception. This concept has to undergo a drastic change.

4. **Readymade Window Sky Lights for Rural Kutcha Mud Houses:** Most of the rural houses which are built out of mud, have a very low roof. This roof further tapers down, in the back portion of the houses. This

portion of the house is always dark and dingy. The occupants sometimes use this part of the house for their sleeping. Light and ventilation is very poor here. As the mobility of the rural population is generally very less, most of the families, therefore, spend several years of their lives, living in this typical enclosure of space-dark and dingy settlement, with very little head room and almost no ventilation.

Readymade windows with vertical bars of the size 60 cm length and 15 cm width, can be mass produced for being used in these unventilated portions of the rural houses. There should be long projection of the length of these windows on both sides, so that they can be securely embedded into the mud wall. On the outer side of the window, there should be a lid suspended from the top. This lid can be kept closed or opened in different angles depending on the requirement of the season. In winter, for instance, this lid can be opened only slightly at night, to prevent cold wind from entering the house. The same procedure can be adopted during the day time in summer to keep out the hot wind.

It must be realised, that rebuilding the rural houses on the urban pattern is a distant dream. To give relief to the rural masses, their houses can be given some device like the windows suggested here, to bring about a quantum improvement in their living standards. Because of the projections of the window on both sides, they will not be easily removable. The security of the house would thus not be affected and at the same time, lighting and the ventilation of the house will be greatly improved.

5. **Corrugated Galvanized Iron (CGI) Sheets for Roofs:** CGI sheets are useful materials for the roof of rural houses. In the planes of north, central and south India, they have, however, limited utility, because the summer temperature in these areas is very high. It becomes unbearable to live under these sheets in these regions. In north eastern states, however, there is a great demand of these sheets, because temperatures never go very high. The sheets are very good protection against heavy rainfall of these regions. Painted with red-oxide paint, such sheets have a fairly long life.

There is a good case, for setting up of specialised steel plants in the North-East, to produce these sheets. Any visitor to Assam or any other state of the North-East will encounter a large number of houses built with CGI sheet roofs. The special needs of this much neglected region ought to be satisfied by arranging abundent supply of these sheets. It is strange, that this matter has never caught the attention of our economic planners.

6. **Supply of Cattle Feed:** There is a great need of providing healthy cattle feed in rural areas. The milch animals fail to produce milk to their full capacity in the absence of some rare elements. It is, therefore, necessary that plentiful supply of balanced fodder-supplements for the animals of the cultivator should be ensured. Small dosages of those elements or compounds which trigger production of milk to the total milk yielding capability of the cows and buffalos should be readily available in the rural areas. This will also give strength to the draft animals. In addition, salt-licks containing these rare but vital elements and compounds should be mass produced. They are

61

suspended by a chain in front of the cattle that go on licking them as per their need. In a predominantly agricultural country, such things should be available in abundance, at a reasonable price. At present, factory produced cattle feed is looked upon as an elitist item. The needs of the urban area should not overshadow, the urgent needs of the rural areas.

Improved Consumption—The Real Test of Removal of Poverty

Whenever and wherever, one thinks of removal of poverty, improved consumption of goods and services, comes to mind as the real indicator of its removal. Consumerism is decried by some people, as the bane of the modern society. In India, in particular, there has been a general opinion against consumerism. The idols set up by our time-honoured saints, always emphasized the merit of leading a life in which people could make do with as little as possible use of the worldly things. Mahatma Gandhi set an example of the same tradition of Indian ethos. He, however, said that there is enough for everybody's needs but not enough for everyone's greed.

Time has come now, to give everyone according to his needs. The classical definitions of Socialism and Communism may be profitably reproduced here. Socialism envisages *From Each According to His Capacity and to Each According to His Work*. Communism on the other hand goes a step beyond this and postulates that *From Each According to His Capacity and to Each According to His Needs*. The third and the final stage of communist thinking, is the *Withering Away of the State*.

The socialistic ideology is that everyone should be engaged in the production of goods and services and in return

62

everyone should get, only what one deserves to get for ones labour.

According to the classical theory of communism, if everyone works for four hours every day, there will be so much production of goods and services that everyone can be provided with enough of these goods and services to meet ones needs. Finally, this theory presumes, that there will be such a plenty of goods and services in the world that they will be as freely available as air and light. Just as, no one tries to acquire or capture air and sunlight, so also none will be tempted to grab the goods and services because they will be available to everyone in plenty. At this stage, the institution called STATE, will no longer be required to exist. In this Utopia of the leftist ideology, there will no more be any disputes about the acquisition or possession of property. No machinery of the state would therefore be needed then. This would be 'The Withering Away of the State'.

The above thesis of the communist way of thinking does not match with the principles on which the free world countries run their society. Even in the case of the Soviet Union, this ideology ultimately failed and Russia, the remnant of the erstwhile Soviet Union, has returned to a near capitalist way of running the country. While there is a regimentation in the society of the communist pattern, China has taken to trading like a capitalist country. Thus, China has made a very successful amalgamation of the communist ideology with capitalism.

In any case, India is least likely to take to the leftist way of running the society. There is deep seated faith in religion, and the leftist way of thinking is a taboo. Further, the country is predominantly an agricultural society. Every

63

owner of a piece of agricultural land holds his proprietorship of his land very dear to his heart. Individual freedom is jealously guarded against any attempt to disturb it.

With the above noted traits, India is going to remain a free world country. To preserve this free society, the country has to take urgent steps to alleviate poverty and uplift the rural masses to a respectable standard of living.

Generating Employment Opportunities

By bringing about disinvestment in the existing public sector industries, we will be drawing the resources of the general public in their running. There are 214 centrally owned public sector companies, of which only 160 are profit making. The rest have been making losses for years. By disinvestment, the government intends to make these Public Sector Undertakings (PSUs) benefit from techno–managerial efficiencies and become more competitive in the market.

The resources generated from this offloading of shares of the PSUs should go to create new industrial ventures, devoted to the production of goods for villagers. These new industries will also open up, vast opportunities for employment. This will be in addition to the employment provided by the existing industries which are intended to be partly opened up for public share. In this way, there will be a new chain of industrial units which will again provide avenues for generating employment. A very serious problem before the country is that of unemployment. With the existing industrial units, the possibilities of increasing employment are virtually negligible. When, on the other hand, new groups of industries dot the face of the country, there will be a great spurt in the field of employment.

As has been discussed earlier, such industrial establishments should be located in small towns, thereby providing opportunities to the rural youth of the surrounding rural areas, to get engaged in these ventures. Actually, this will avoid the crowding and pollution, generally associated with large industrial centers.

As things stand, we do not have any clue as to how to tackle the grave problem of unemployment. It is on a high path with the increase in population. Some of the measures suggested here provide us with a chance to face and solve this problem. The reinvestment of the funds raised from the disinvestment of the existing industries can give us a historical chance to create conditions of maximum employment. Side by side, we will be generating items of immediate utility for the rural people, who have suffered deprivation from times immemorial. While these people will get a chance to lift themselves from their abysmal poverty, the unemployed in turn, will get an opportunity for gainful employment. This will be, in a way, India's "Great Leap Forward".

Strong political will is required, for taking this bold untraditional step. This massive revolutionary action in favour of the rural poor can take place only when there is a determined resolve to bring up the ever suffering, ever poor and ever deprived people, living in the villages to a reasonably high and comfortable standard of living.

Opportunities to take bold steps to revolutionise the economic structure of the country present themselves only once in centuries. Such changes in the positive direction are indeed very rare. In the negative direction, such changes are forced upon the nation when faced with a war like situation. The whole society gears itself up, to accepting drastic changes. People are more than ready to put up with withdrawal of the usual supplies and facilities. During a war, employment levels reach to their maximum. The wheels of industry run round the clock. The public enthusiasm reaches the level of frenzy. Why can't we create the same physical and emotional conditions, when we undertake the task of changing the face of the countryside?

❑❑❑

7   Making Goods for the Rural Citizens

It is said that man does not live by bread alone. On the same analogy, one should expect that the people of the rural areas will like to avail of many items which go to make their lives more convenient and pleasant. The rural people can't be denied for long, those items of good living which are used by the urban people to make their lives brighter. Such items may fall in the category of luxury. Nevertheless, there is a need for these items in a rural household. With better earnings, the average villager may himself arrange to buy such goods from the nearby urban market. What we should aim here, is to make these things available at or near the village.

A noted economist Say has postulated a theory that 'supply creates its own demand'. By this maxim, we may infer that if such items become readily available at a reasonable price, the rural consumer will surely go for them. Whatever money he can save or arrange from some source, would then be diverted to the purchase of these non-essential but useful items.

In making an inventory of such goods, the most prominent requirement appears to be of items made of plastics. The urban people have gone whole hog for plastic products in their daily life. With gradual improvement in products of the Petro Chemical industry, the urban homes are replete with plastic goods. They are light, strongly built and easily maneuverable. It is true that they suffer from the great handicap, that they are not bio-degradable nor can they be easily recycled, as facilities for the same are not readily available. Despite these drawbacks, the use of plastics has been steadily increasing in the urban sector of society. There is, in particular, a strong opinion against carry bags, made of thin plastic sheets because they clog the drainage, and cause fatal problems for the cattle who unwittingly try to swallow them. We may, therefore, avoid sending these kind of items, to the rural market. What can be safely made available to them would be, plastic buckets, mugs, kitchen containers and plastic sheets, for covering the heaps of food grains, chemicals and fertilizers etc. used for agricultural purposes.

The rural children also deserve to have toys to play with. The childhood urge to handle toys must be recognised and should be made available at low cost. Toys of a rough and tough make, ought to be made available in the rural area. The measure of happiness, which these toys generate in the tender minds of children, is unfathomable. When our aim is to create overall happiness amongst the village people, we cannot afford to ignore the claims of the children over such happiness. Parental love, flows with as much intensity in the rural setting as in an urban area. A delicate handling of the children in their tender age, goes a long way to make the same child, a sympathetic and sensitive adult. Neglect and rough handling, begets the same lack of sensitivity in the adult. By providing toys and other play things, let us make an attempt to breed our rural children in an appropriate sympathetic atmosphere.

Besides children, the women of the rural area also need attention so as to satisfy their natural urge for good looks. Women, young and old, care a lot for their personal appearance. In young women, the attractive appearance plays an important role, ensuring a happy bondage between the husband and wife. Neglected personal appearance, results in apathy between them. While the urban markets are now overflowing with lucrative aids and recipes for beauty enhancement, no such attention is paid to the 35 per cent or so of the national population, the rural women. The manufacturers of beauty aids, need to be induced to adequately cover the requirements, of this rural female population. The beauty products sold to this sector should be reasonably priced but equally important, the standard of the product should also be maintained and should meet the demands and aspirations of the rural women. The younger section of this rural society of women is ready to welcome such products. With the spread of educational facilities, these girls are fast picking up the modern ways of dressing, make up and living.

Some other non-essential, but useful items can be listed here. They include Hurricane Lanterns, torches with cells or re-chargeable type, incandescent lamps of the type sold under the trade name of 'Aladin's Lamp' (which has round wicks, over which an incandescent filament is kept, to generate a bright light, like Petromax). The list can be extended to include several other utility items, having place in a rural household.

The old people of the rural area are looked after by the rest of the family with a fair amount of care and attention. The bonds of love and affection still persist in the rural families. Besides, the sense of respect for the elderly and the economic factor also plays its role. The agricultural land holdings are normally recorded in the name of the eldest member of the family. Unless partition of such holdings is done on the demand of the youngsters or rarely, on the initiative of the head of the family, the joint agricultural property which is the main source of income for the family, remains under the command of the head of the family.

Institutional care of senior citizens, is a far cry in the rural setting. Sons, daughters-in-law and grandchildren combine together to attend to their grandparents. Sometimes, there is a reservation in the mind of the daughters-in-law in this matter because they come from outside the family but very soon they fall in line with the rest of their new family members on realizing the fact that the rights over the property are still vested in the head of the family.

If we take an account, of the day to day physical needs of the elderly citizens of the village, we come across a few items which can make their life happy and safe. Most of the elderly people use a staff or a long and strong stick for support, when they walk around. When they become too old, to move about with the help of a stick, they very much need the "Walker". This is a metallic stand by the support of which, old and crippled people can slowly walk for short distances. Folding type of Walkers are available which can be conveniently carried and stored. They are a vital need of the family.

The next important item for the welfare of the rural people is the supply of anti-mosquito measures. The most dependable and totally safe thing, is the mosquito net. It acts as a protection against mosquitoes and other insects as well. If properly tucked under the bed-sheets, it provides protection against snakes and scorpions too. Cheap type of mosquito nets, can be made out of a strong cellular fabric. The personnel of the armed forces are issued with such type of nets and they use them even while sleeping on the ground. The villagers can muster a cot, for using them in a regular way or they may tie the long strands in the nails, dug in the walls. Flexible bamboo sticks are also used in putting up these nets, the bamboo sticks are affixed to the legs of the cot in a 'x' shape and are kept in a position by the four strings of the mosquito net.

Some more items which can be thought of, for supply to the rural elders, include spectacles and dentures. This calls for the existence of primary health care centres, within easy reach of the villagers. The scheme of conducting Cataract operations in eye camps is proving to be a great boon to the old people of the villages. They used to suffer from this degenerative disease of the eye for years in the evening of their lives till such a campaign was set in motion. There may have been occasional failures of these eye operations. By and large, however, they have brought a wonderful relief to the senior citizens of the villages.

As for dental care, it is noticed that village elders accept the fall of their teeth, as an inevitable consequence of growing age. When they suffer from shooting pain in their teeth, they resort to the crude operation of pulling out of the ailing tooth by quacks. Replacing the lost teeth by an artificial denture, is still a far cry for them. Let alone the rural area, dental treatment is a very costly affair in the urban areas also. One of the reasons for this, is the shortage of qualified dental surgeons. The BDS course, preparing these doctors is a costly and long drawn training course, lasting four years, for covering all aspects of oral diseases. The need of the villagers is, however, to have simple dentists trained within a year or so, who should be able to provide relief needed by old people. This calls for a condensed course on dental care. The products of these courses, can be deployed in the Primary Health Centers. If there is any need for specialised treatment, such patients could be referred to the next higher Health Care Unit. Leaving the rural area, totally out of the coverage of the dental care services (as is happening now), is a matter of great concern. The total health of a person is determined, in a large measure, by the health of his teeth. The condition of the urban poor is better in this regard. Here the name of Aneyurin Bevan comes to mind. He was the architect of the Health Insurance Scheme of Britain, as the Minister of Public Health in Clement Atlee's cabinet. Later, he moved on to become the Minister of Labour. He resigned from his post in 1951 when free supply of dentures and spectacles was not included in the package of State Health Insurance. Those people who have had the misfortune of suffereing from toothache, can very well realise the value of the services of a dentist.

❑❑❑

Why "Making Goods for Villagers"

It is a pertinent question to ask, why we should delve in the issue of, making things for villagers. It can be argued that the rural people have lived for centuries with the facilities and handicaps available to them. It can also be said that they have reached a state of equilibrium, with the situation they are in. Men, women, young and old, boys and girls as well as the children, have come to regard the rural setting of their lives, as something unalterable. Being, by and large, unaware of the blessings of the goods used and availed of by the urban people, they do not pine for what is not available to them?

The question arises, should we leave them to their fate and satisfy ourselves, by assuming that the present day situation with which they have come to strike an adjustment, is their destiny. Here, one is reminded of the theory of Dr. Verier Ellwyn. As an expert on tribal culture and way of life, he advised the government not to disturb the setting in which the tribal people lived. During the Prime Ministership of Pt. Jawaharlal Nehru, this theory came to be accepted as a policy of Government for the tribal population of India. Dr. Verier Ellwyn was, perhaps, right in his thinking, in a way. His perception was, that after arousing the ambitions of the tribal people to achieve a modern way of advanced society, it may not be possible to fulfil their aspirations.

Such a situation, actually arose in the State of Arunachal Pradesh. Before the new State was formed, this remote area of North-East was known as the North East Frontier Agency or NEFA. This area was administered by the Governor of Assam. The security advisor to the Governor, was in the actual charge of administering the territory, spread out from Burma (now Myanmar) on the east to Bhutan on the west. Col. K.A.A. Raja, the last Security Advisor of NEFA and the first Lieutenant Governor of Arunachal Pradesh, used to take very keen interest in the development of NEFA. As a part of his welfare measures, he organised tours of the tribal people of NEFA, to the rest of India. The result of this step taken with the best of intentions, was very counter-productive. On return from the tour of cities like Bombay, Delhi and Calcutta, the tribal tourists became highly agitated. They angrily complained that they had been totally denied the benefits enjoyed by the people of the rest of the country. Such tours had to be ultimately abandoned.

In the case of the rural masses, a similar situation can arise some day. With the spread of education and the empowering of the village level administrative units, like Gram Panchayats, the rural people will no longer accept the denial of the benefits of urban living to them. In fact, there are two ways of looking at the problem of uplifting the backward rural area. One is to bring them on par with the advanced areas of the country, by the process of gradual supply of better amenities and providing better conditions of living. This may be called the 'Development on As-is-Where is basis'. The other method would be, to bring about a revolution in these backward areas for a drastic and wholesale change in the conditions of these areas. This method has already been adopted by Government in some of the naxalite affected states.

Whether such violent revolutions, do actually bring about the desired change, is still an open question. This method may ultimately lead to equal distribution of poverty rather than equitable distribution of prosperity.

The greatest revolution in the world, was brought about by the Bolsheviks in Russia, ruled by Czars. The inspiration for this upheaval was drawn from the book 'Das Capital', written by Karl Marx which was written by him in the library of the British Museum of London. Ultimately his ideas were adopted and implemented by the Communist Regime of Russia. Thereafter, despite several efforts to export the communists ideology to other countries, a large section of the world remained non-communist. Several countries like the Britain, countries of the Western Europe etc. did not convert themselves into the communist way of running the society.

It has been remarked that these countries were not converted into the communist way of life because, "A man called Karl Marx wrote a book called Das Capital and it was read by the countries of the free world". These nations adopted several points from this book to change their society in such a way that adopting a totalitarian regime, was no longer necessary.

Measures like, Social Security schemes, unemployment benefits to the unemployed, food tickets for the needy, state health insurance etc. were adopted which made irrelevant the introduction of the harsh steps associated with Communism.

It is high time for India, to take a lesson from these free-world countries. The deprived sections of Indian Society, residing in the rural areas should be uplifted from their poverty stricken way of life. What the communists wanted to achieve by a wholesale revolt in the society, should be achieved by providing small dosages of relief to the poor. An atmosphere should be created in which the rural masses feel that they are being cared for by the nation. By making things for villagers, we will be assuaging their ruffled feelings.

Attempts of the neighboring countries, to foment trouble in our homeland by instigating the tribal people and the poorer sections of the rural society, can be counteracted by meeting the aspirations of these deprived sections of the society.

Efforts have to be made on a mass scale, in the form of a campaign, to produce and supply such goods and services which meet the needs of the villagers at least half-way. The present system, of passing on to them only the surplus left over of Industrial goods after their supply to the urban area, will not succeed in stopping the minds of deprived rural masses, from resorting to violent methods of bringing about a change in their conditions. Let us hear the battle-cries of the left ultras, who are bent upon exploiting the despair and anguish of the rural people, especially the people belonging to aboriginal tribes, to start a movement for the total overthrow of the established society. These deprived people prove a fertile ground for sowing seeds of dissatisfaction with the present establishment. Attempts to suppress such movements, by treating this as a matter of law and order only can't succeed, unless, side by side, we launch a campaign to provide succour to these sections of the society. Handling such attempts of the radical sections of certain political parties with a firm hand will prove counterproductive, if measures to ameliorate the living conditions of the vast majority of our population living in the tribal and rural areas, are not taken along with the suppression of the armed rebellion. An attempt has been made in the previous chapter of this book to suggest ways of uplifting the living standard of the rural masses by injecting small but effective dosages of relief.

It is realised that there cannot be a magic wand by which the rural scene may be transformed within a short time, which is available to us, to counter the pressure of the rebellious elements of a radical political ideology. What is, however, possible is to produce things for villagers to provide them immediate solace.

❑❑❑

9   Funds for Making Things for Villagers

In an ideal society, the consumers are the prime movers of the wheels of industry. The more the people consume, more is the production and in turn there is greater generation of employment. A cycle of consumption, production and employment, has to be set in motion.

A fundamental question arises here from where are the financial resources expected to come for initiating this cycle? Notionally speaking, goods have to be produced first, before they go to the consumer, who in turn lends support to this cycle by paying for the goods. Lastly, the earnings from the sale of goods, generates employment.

The initial funding of industries, producing the goods for villagers, must be done by the resources of the State. After setting the cycle of consumption, production and employment in motion, the State funding agency may expect to gradually withdraw from this activity, leaving the running of this cycle, to its own momentum. Now, the big question is, wherefrom the funds for initiating such a process are to come.

A large number of Public Sector Undertakings (PSUs) have been set-up in our country to meet the basic needs of the society. They have gone on to produce electricity, heavy electricals, fertilizers and several other items, normally not produced by the private sector. Some of them have been profit making, while others have been losing concerns. Very recently, the Central Government has given an indication, that it may go in for divesting its share from the PSUs. About 25 per cent of equities of these units, is intended to be offered to the public for raising funds. When leftists were a vital part of the ruling coalition, they had insisted that the State run industry should be preserved and supported. If Government decided to disinvest the shares of these PSUs, it was incumbent upon the Government, to put the money so earned by this method, in a separate fund called National Investment Fund (NIF). This fund could not be used to close the fiscal deficit or to fund expenditure on social and infrastructure sectors. The NIF was supposed to be used for retraining workers facing retrenchment and rehabilitating sick PSUs. Under the stringent rules of the NIF, the government had agreed not to touch the corpus of the fund. Instead it used the income earned from interest only for select social sector schemes and a quarter of it for meeting capital investments in revival of PSUs. "There is now a clear understanding in the government to move ahead on disinvestments". It would go in for sale of equity in listed PSUs, so that they have at least 25 per cent public holding. That would create enough resources for funding the government's key projects and flagship schemes. (A copy of the news item published in Times of India, Bombay Edition on 8th July, 2009 is included here as Appendix–II.)

The most essential and laudable projects to be funded from such funds originally held under the classification of NIF, would be to use them for setting up industries, to produce goods for the villagers.

❑❑❑

10 "Relevant Portion of the Text of the Finance Minister's Speech Delivered on Tuesday the 7ᵗʰ July, 2009"

"My ministry has initiated discussions with other ministries to identify public sector undertakings, where a portion of government shareholding in PSUs could be sold to meet fund requirement," he said in the Lok Sabha on Tuesday, while replying to the debate on Budget 2009–10. "Details are being worked out and could be announced in due course."

Officials indicated that the government plans to list profitable Central Public Sector Undertakings (CPSUs), each with a net worth of over Rs. 200 crore, and equity divestment would be done by floating an Initial Public Offering (IPO), either independently by the government in conjunction with a fresh equity issue or the company concerned.

There are 214 centrally-owned public sector companies, of which only 160 are profit-making. The rest have been making losses for years.

"It is our intention to enable PSUs to benefit from techno-managerial efficiencies and become more competitive in the market," Mukherjee said.

He said there was "disappointment" that the budget did not give details of the government's disinvestment agenda. In a way, this leaves options before the government, about the utilisation of the disinvestment funds. The compulsions of the National Investment Fund (NIF), no longer restrict these options to particular items of utilisation, like the training of retrenched workers, as a result of disinvestment. After the withdrawal of influence and pressure of the leftists, the central government is now free to choose the method of utilising disinvestment funds.

One of the options under considerations appears to be, to bridge the fiscal deficit in the current budget of 2009-2010. In the traditional way of managing the financial affairs of the country, deficit financing is usually considered to be something which ought to be avoided. This is expected to put the economy in an inflationary mode.

Fortunately, at the present time, inflation has almost disappeared and the urgency to bridge the deficit in the budget, is therefore, not a priority. The other option discussed hereafter, calls for an urgent attention, due to very pressing needs of the nation, at the present juncture.

On taking stock as of the entire situation of the country, of which maintenance of law and order, in face of the onslaught of the Maoist type of leftist violence, there can't be a better option, than to invest these funds in improving the lot of the rural masses. While defending the society against such attacks of Maoists by the security forces, the positive activity of ameliorating the dire and stark poverty of the tribal and other backward population of the rural areas is an equally important step. Unless these two strategies go on side by side simultaneously, it will be difficult to control the leftist sponsored violence.

Nations get very rare opportunity to take up a wholesale restructuring of the economic fabric of the country. With the funds available with the government because of disinvestment, such an opportunity has presented itself in a historical epoch. Bold steps are required to be taken, to seize this rare chance in the history of the nation. A massive diversion of public funds, for making things for the villagers, may prove to be a turning point in the development of the country.

If we miss this opportunity, we may be missing a rarest of the rare chances, to uplift the rural masses. We have gone on crying, about the resource crunch for decades and centuries, when it comes to spending for the rural areas. The urban areas have always had the cake. The insatiable hunger of the urban sector, will never allow the government to find enough funds for mass scale and quantum changes in the conditions of the rural people.

It is true, that the rural people have the power of votes in their favour. The management of the government however, is in the hands of the urban people. Few of them, have ever experienced the troubles and travails of a rural household. Even a slight deprivation of amenities, upsets the urban people. On the other hand, a permanent denial of such basic facilities, like leak-proof roofs, ventilated and well-lit living space, clean spot in the house for cooking, arrangement for a mosquito-free sleep, have never pinched the conscience of the urban managers of rural affairs. Like the saying "East is East and West is West", the twin shall never meet. The urban planner will always remain an unconcerned decider of the fate of rural people and so the poor villager will always continue to live in perpetual abject poverty. As has been stated above, the removal of poverty comes through better consumption of goods and services. To change the fate of the villager, seeped in utter deprivation for centuries, a campaign to make things for him, has to be launched. Nothing short of this, can ever banish poverty from the face of India (or any other country having poor rural masses).

The disinvestment funds should, therefore, be ploughed-back into the economy, to setup factories turning out goods for rural consumption. Such goods may have to be branded as "For Rural Consumption Only". A series of measures like tax holiday, supply of power at concessional rates, making land available at a nominal price and similar other steps may have to be taken, to give a kick-start to such industrial establishments. They have to be fondly nurtured and supported. The leakage of their products to unintended sectors should be stopped. Even relaxing the labour laws in favour of such enterprises may have to be considered in the larger interest of the society.

The strategy in short will be, to disinvest in the existing industrial units and utilise the funds so raised, to finance new industrial units devoted to the production of things for the villagers.

❑❑❑

11 Some Relevant Indicators of Rural Economy

The Fast Moving Consumer Goods (FMCG) sector, the fourth largest sector in the Indian economy, is counting heavily on the purchasing power of the rural Indian to help it grow at a projected 40 per cent in the future. This is despite the fact that rural indebtedness remains ominously unchanged. It is reported that only 27 per cent of farmers have access to formal credit and the rest rely on private moneylenders. And the fact that along with unviable farm economics, factors like monsoon delay or crop failure make the life of a rural Indian too risky to think of expenditure instead of saving.

It is noteworthy, however, that the Conditional Cash Transfer (CCT) scheme is gathering support as a replacement for a plethora of rural welfare measures. This scheme proposes that the government will deposit an amount in the account of the beneficiaries identified according to poverty criteria. The amount is deposited in the name of the woman member of the household and accessed only if children go to school or attend the health centre. Along with the National Rural Employment Guarantee Scheme (NREGS), loan waivers and increase in prices at which agricultural products are sold, bring in disposable incomes lying untapped in the rural area for improved consumption by farmers. The idea of the FMCG industries is to give a choice to the rural consumer to shift to branded products from traditional unbranded merchandise from the non organised sector. It is surmised that rural India constitutes over 60 per cent of the country's total consumer base. It is estimated that rural markets hold 55 per cent of total LIC policies, 50 per cent of the market for televisions, fans, bicycles and wristwatches and a massive 70 per cent of the market for toilet soap consumption. The sale and use of the Mobile Phones appears to have matched the number of phones used in the urban area.

This picture of rural sales and consumption of industrial goods is the position when there is no supply of tailor-made products for the rural consumers. If we undertake the production of such items which are specifically designed to suit the needs, purchasing power, maintenance capability and, above all, the fancy of the rural masses, the share of the rural consumption will go up several times.

The economic survey of 2007–08 says rural India spends, on average, 55 per cent on foods and a substantial 45 per cent on non-food items like clothing, consumer durables, education and health. Its spending on items which add to the cost of living in urban area such as electricity, transport, fuel and rent is negligible. Factors, like this have created disposable incomes which the rural consumer should be, ideally, keen on spending on consumer goods. Thus, it appears that there are disposable incomes lying untapped in rural India. If the rural population spends some of this, it will act as an engine of progress to take the country out of the age old scenario of deprivations and despair.

Keynesian economics which pulled out Britain from the evil effects of the World War II postulates that government should become the prime-mover of the economic process.

Spending by government has a multiplier effect. A bold step of setting up industries dedicated to serve the rural market can bring about the end of inertia which has beset itself on the rural countryside for centuries.

❑❑❑

12 Problem in Setting up Industries in Rural Area

In putting up any factory in a rural area, one faces problems, many of which are the outcome of the psychology of the rural people. Despite the benefits galore, a common man owning land gets upset, if his land is acquired for such a project. It is a delicate task to ensure the acceptance among villagers, to allow industry to be setup in the rural areas. The experience of setting up Special Economic Zones (SEZ), has not been a pleasant one and the scheme appears to have been totally shelved because it raised violent protests, in the states of West Bengal and Gujarat. In India, acquisition of agricultural land is a very sensitive issue. There are millions of people, whose livelihood depends on agricultural land. The introduction of SEZs in India, has resulted in the dispossession of cultivated areas and has affected the livelihood of the farmers, at large. Farmers first protested to safeguard their interests, through litigation and court cases, challenging the establishment of SEZs. But later on, the resistance against SEZ became massive when political parties also joined the in fray. There were two glaring incidents of clash between the farmers and the government. The first one was at Jamnagar in Gujarat, with the Reliance Industries. They moved the High Court of Gujarat and later the Supreme Court, to say that the setting up of SEZs, violated not only the Land Acquisition Act of 1894 but was also in breach of the public interest. This led the Government, to consider putting a ceiling on the maximum land area, that can be acquired for multi product zones and decided to go slow in approving SEZs.

In the case of West Bengal, the SEZ proposed to be set up at village Nandigram in Purba Medinipur district, located 70 Kms south-west of Kolkata, opposite the industrial city of Haldia aroused a much more violent protest from the farmers. West Bengal government, (headed by the Leftists) allotted 10,000 acres of land for a SEZ to be developed by the Indonesia-based Salim Group to set up a chemical hub. It is reported that a police party of more than 3000 heavily armed policemen stormed the Nandigram area and shot dead 14 villagers and wounded 70 more including children and women.

The above examples shows that these SEZs started with a lot of premature praise and poor preparation became a bone of contention and which was readily exploited by the political forces to the detriment of the peasants, who fear losing their means of livelihood.

In planning the industrial enterprises to produce things for the villagers, the above noted pitfalls will have to be carefully avoided. First and foremost, the villagers who lose their cultivable land for such projects, will have to be informed that the projects are for the benefit for their own class. In both the above noted extreme cases, the villagers found outside capitalist parties taking possession of their land. The ultimate purpose of the enterprises being set up there didn't enthuse the farmers to sacrifice their land. In one case there was a giant Indian industrialist, the Reliance Group and in the other case a foreign entrepreneur. In both the cases, not even a remote or direct benefit was seen to be coming to the dispossessed village community. To generate a willing surrender of their land, the cultivators owning the land will have to be properly motivated. An outline of the entire scheme of "Making Goods for Villagers" will have to be explained to them. Information and publicity will have to be taken in the form of a campaign. The villagers affected by the acquisition of their land should have an emotional fervour to contribute their might in this revolutionary change.

Let us remember, how people, high and low, come forward willingly and voluntarily for great personal sacrifices when a call is given for saving the nation from a foreign attack. The same psychic frenzy should be generated amongst the rural population when they are being called upon to fight against their age-old backwardness and eternal poverty. When a lead is given in this direction by some socially oriented villagers, others will emulate their example. One may recall the stupendous task of merging the Princely States, numbering about 550, achieved by the Iron-man of India, Sardar Vallabhbhai Patel. Ably added by his associate V.P. Menon, he set up leaders among the princes to show the path of merger with the Indian Union. Following the examples set by such rulers, all the willing and even unwilling Rulers of the Indian Princely States fell in a line to agree to sign the Instrument of Merger. It is reported by V.P. Menon that the entire process of the merger of States started at Cuttack (Orissa). The Ruler of Dehnkenal agreed to sign the merger after which the other Rulers of Orissa decided to follow his example. With the instrument of merger given by the Orissa Princes, in his pocket, Sardar Vallabhbhai Patel came to Nagpur where he showed these letters to the Rulers of the Chhattisgarh States. They also followed the lead given earlier by their peers. A chain reaction was set in motion and within months the entire fraternity of Indian Princes had agreed to merge their territories into the Indian Union with two great exceptions of the Nizam of Hyderabad and the Maharaja of Kashmir. Sardar Patel launched a military attack which was termed as "Police action" and ensured the merger of the Nizam's territory into India. For reasons best known to him, Pandit Jawaharlal Nehru did not allow the Sardar to handle the Kashmir case and as a result the problem of Kashmir has continued to be a source of great distress and despair for India.

The above example shows that people usually fall in line when someone gives a lead and other people follow the line. Coming to a campaign concern with land reforms, named as Bhoodan-yagya started by the great Gandhian leader Vinoba Bhave, astonishing success was achieved in securing the donation of land from large land holders all over the country in favour of the landless. In the absence of a vigorous follow up, the Bhoodan movement could not be sustained. The great Gandhian, Vinoba conducted the country-wide agitation by taking long walks-Pad-Yatra. In any case, the enthusiasm generated a nationwide responses extending from Assam to the central India owners of large area land were vying with each other to register their donations. If the campaign had been conducted in a efficient modern way and if there were leaders behind Vinoba to support the movement it would have brought about a silent revolution of land reforms. No doubt, it is today a much forgotten campaign.

The acquisitions of land for setting up factories making goods for the villagers will surely pose serious problems. The troubles faced by SEZ is an indicator that a great caution will be required in handling this issue. The first thing which can ease the situation is to have wide publicity of the fact that the factories being established will turn out goods for the direct benefit of the villagers themselves. They should be motivated to think themselves as partners in this movement. In the case of SEZs, the land-losers had no direct benefit to themselves. The beneficiaries in this case were capitalist of Indian and even foreign origin.

Further, the land losers should be compensated not only fairly and adequately, but also liberally and even lavishly. The present system of awarding compensation on the basis of the value of land as recorded in the documents of the registration of earlier year, is fraught with severe injustice to the land losers. It is well-known as the land transactions are registered with the government agency at a value far below the actual price paid for the land in order to save the stamp duty and registration charges. Land acquisition by government is dreaded by land owners due to this procedure. We will have to device some more just and fair way of compensating the land owner for the land taken from him. Calculation on the basis of the value indicated by the figures obtained from the Registration of transaction can be safely multiplied four times to secure a willing surrender of land for a good public cause. In fact, land prices have been souring up so fast that adopting this procedure should not be treated as a case of misplaced bounty.

The second action to solve the land problem should be to offer employment on priority basis to the land losers and their dependents. In the case of the land acquisition for the Narmada Valley Development Authority (NVDA) in Madhya Pradesh, several villagers who were dispossessed from their land for the construction of the NVDA project have felt that they have gained and not lost by giving their land. In place of their poor lands, they have moved out to new locations which are in or near the urban settlements.

Their children have done better than what they could have done in their own earlier locations. The setting up of manufacturing facilities near the homes of the land-losers will surely bring in a new wind of development and modernization. There will be better facilities of transport, education, health care and trade and commerce as a follow up of the setting up of these factories. Instead of the usual migration from the villages to the urban areas, this activity will, in a way, take the urban area facilities to the rural masses. This is in addition to making goods for villagers—a larger and more fundamental objective of this activity.

Lastly, if everything failed in persuading some obstinate and stubborn land owners to part with their land willingly, the stiff policy of compulsory land acquisition will have to be resorted to. Liberal compensation for the acquired land will perhaps assuage their feelings. The procedure adopted should be quick and efficient. Unscrupulous Revenue Officers and middle-men must not be allowed to dabble in the land acquisition cases. Land Acquision Officer should dispose off cases on the spot with the immediate payment of compensation by cheques. One very important item of expenditure will be of securing or acquiring land for such establishment.

Despite all efforts to avoid resistance or bitterness, land acquisition may generate negative feelings among some of the people affected. It will require a high degree of tact and diligence to prevent this negativity from becoming a mass-movement. The sensitization of the land-losers should be so effective that the political parties may not be able to exploit them for their agitation. There should be Information Offices, Call Centers, and Public Grievance Removal Centers for receiving the complaints and doubts from the local people. They should not feel the need to seek the support of political workers or resort to an agitation.

The village people who are affected by the acquisition of their land for setting up such factories should feel that they are doing their sacrifice for producing their own items and providing employment to their own people. Shares of the company set up should be sold to these people on a limited scale to make them feel their participation in the ownership of the factories.

In short, the activity of setting up such industries in rural areas should be indigenous and participative. It should be indigenous in the sense it should produce items which are of direct use in enriching the life of the villagers themselves. The workers should feel proud that they are engaged in self-help in a big way. It should be participative in the sense that it should provide employment to the people of the area surrounding the industrial establishment.

Removing poverty from the rural area constituting about 70 per cent of India is a gigantic task. It cannot be achieved by half-hearted efforts. Despite the power of vote available with the rural masses, the arbiters of their fate are still the people of the urban areas.

In its ultimate analysis, removal of poverty is essentially improving the consumption level of goods and services of people. These should be made available to the rural people as an initial step to uplift them from their age-old deprivation. It is the 'Supply-side Economics' that will change the face of the countryside.

Instead of providing better living conditions, villagers have been given sermons to live in simplicity and produce more and more agricultural products for the country. There is almost no quid-pro-quo from the urban sector to the rural masses who are treated as bonded labourers for producing agricultural commodities. Their produce is sold in the market, at a price dictated by urban business magnates or by Government. There is a system in vogue of fixing administered prices for most of the agricultural commodities. *At this rate, the rural people will be perpetually poor.*

To break this deadlock, drastic steps need to be taken to usher in a new Industrial Revolution. MAKING GOODS FOR VILLAGERS should be the Mantra of this new Udyog Yagya. Let us take a bold initiative to take the country forward.

A major factor of the social environment and mental make up of the villagers, is that cash loans given to them mostly go astray. The presumption that such credits advanced to the villager, will go directly towards improving his cultivation, has been belied time and again. Instead of advancing cash loans, items of utility, which go to improve agriculture practices and the living conditions of the farmers are needed.

Concerted gigantic efforts will have to be made to make the men and women behind the plough, healthy robust people, living in reasonably comfortable conditions.

The funds for such a revolutionary step, must be found from our healthy accumulation of foreign reserves and from the funds generated by dis-investment of our public sector undertakings (PSUs).

The urgency of implementing the suggestions arises, from the incipient but sure progress of Maoists movement, amidst the perpetually deprived rural masses, constituting a vast majority of our nation's population. We are now faced with a situation of 'Do or Die' alternatives.

❏❏❏

Appendix–I

Making Goods For Villagers

We have often heard it being said that India is a rich country where poor people live. In spite of the four five-year plans, envisaging unprecedented economic activity, there has been a continuing stagnation in the economy resulting in unemployment on the one hand and lack of a serious impact on the lives of the millions living in the rural areas on the other.

The root of the malarise lies in the fact that we have not been able to involve the real rural masses in our industrial activity. We have been trying to run a minicycle of production-consumption-employment with the 20 or 30 per cent of the population living in urban or semi-urban areas. The bulk of the people who constitute India are out of this picture of hectic economic activity. Their lives have remained, by and large, untouched and unaffected by what all has been done in the past 20 years of planned industrial revolution.

The centre of our economic activity must be the village-dweller. Until and unless he comes out of his shell, all our efforts to lift the country will fall. As soon as he joins in this enterprises, both as a producer and as a consumer, the rate of growth of the economy will shoot up.

Have we thought of bringing about changes in the daily lives of the rural masses by making available to them goods and services specially suited to their needs? Have we assessed the daily needs of the villagers and made attempt to meet them in a systematic way? What is needed to remedy the economic ills of the country is a village-oriented mass-production programme.

The industrial sector must be geared to produce articles having an immediate utility in the village life. The country's vast industrial resources should be turned towards the villages. Our industries are oriented to produce articles for the urban consumers. If their products also meet the needs of the rural consumer, this is incidental. There is hardly any sizeable sector of our industry devoted to the production of those articles which have a special utility in the villages.

The focal point of our developmental activities has to be the villager. His needs should dictate the nature of our industrial production. The growth of basic industries gains in the export trade and all such economic pursuits should be looked upon as means to an end and not as ends in themselves. These must fit in the general pattern which has the villager at its central point.

The conversion of products of our basic industries into consumers goods specifically needed for the rural masses should be undertaken on a vast scale, both in the public and the private sector. The division of undertakings into public and private sectors can even be replaced by another and more material division of industries into urban-serving and rural-serving industries.

Unless there is a conscious and controlled transfer of our basic material resources for the production of rural oriented consumer goods, the control is not likely to show signs of development. Feeding the urban market alone will not bring about any change in the country's economic condition.

Uncontrolled and unguided, the industries, not only in the private sector but also in the public sector, have a tendency to adopt the urban consumer as their patron. There are several reasons why industries are geared to meet the needs of cities and towns. The first and foremost is the existence of a ready market with a good demand and comparatively better purchasing power.

The villager has to be wooed by the industries. There is no proper marketing agency making available to him the items he needs. He is not served by well-organised advertising media. In spite of his poverty, he has a marginal purchasing power but it remains unused in the absence of items he requires, i.e., items which he can afford to pay for, which he can maintain with his limited resources and which are harmonious with his way of life.

The privately-owned industry is interested primarily in profits but what is disturbing is that the public-sector industries are also engaged in production for the ready urban market. This may be so because they too are judged by their profits and not by the special service content of their production. Thus, no industry will on its own depart from its well-set pattern of goods production to specially cater of the rural masses.

In the long run, this has more damaging effects than merely leaving the rural masses to their centuries-old lot. The goods and services patronized and consumed by the 20 per cent, urban people are limited in quantity. The result is that the price of such goods and services remains at a high level compared to what it would be it they had a wider clientele.

To facilitate a rural orientation of our Industries, their goods and services need not conform to high international standards, so that they can be priced low to have a very broad-based clientele. The industry should go to the level the rural consumer can afford. We cannot have the standard, quality and price of our products unrelated to the needs and the purchasing power of the bulk of the consumers.

The public sector should be the first to set the pace for a new rural industrial revolution in the country by building factories which will turn out products for direct use and consumption in the rural areas. The private sector should be allowed to closely follow and even compete with the public sector. Standardised items of the villager's needs should be worked out and their price range fixed.

Industrial licenses should be freely offered to private entrepreneurs for the manufacture of such goods. The products of our basic industries should be allotted on a priority basis to this rural industrial sector. Unemployed engineering graduates and technicians should be engaged in these factories. Normal development funds, nationalised banks and the Unit Trust of India (UTI) should finance these projects.

A new rural marketing agency should be started to take the products of these factories to the villages. For local sales, the cooperative sector may be tapped, along with the traditional shop-keeper. The village weekly market should receive our close attention and support. There should be an advertising branch under the rural marketing corporation which should inform and guide the rural masses regarding the new goods and services placed in their disposal. The educated unemployed should be engaged in this grass-level reconstruction job.

The green revolution has already improved the lot of the enterprising section of the rural society. As ambitious scheme for providing on a large-scale, employment in the rural areas is being implemented in some parts of the country through crash programmes. It is necessary to follow up these developments with a programme of providing to the villager an opportunity for the proper utilisation of his newly-acquired purchasing power.

The most promising point from which we should set out for the represent less of our economy and for establishing a balance between the rural and urban sectors is the starting of a chain of factories which should turn out products for sale and consumption is rural sector. The inertia of our economy will be broken only when the rural sector is involved in the industrial revolution. The industrial sector will gain momentum only when its products are deliberately and purposefully fed to the rural sector.

The type of change we envisage in the rural people cannot be brought about if we leave the village consumer out of the benefits of the modern industrial products. His standard of living cannot improve if he is left at the mercy of the village artisan whose goods are inefficient and of poor quality. In the new system, when villagers start getting factory-produced goods, the village artisan will have to adopt a new way of life. The traditional blacksmith, turning out iron tyres for bullock-carts, may have to learn the art of water-pump repairing or tractor servicing.

The crux of the matter is that the rural people should no longer be kept dependent on the village artisan for those items which can be produced cheaper and better in factories. They are as much entitled to the benefits of the large-scale industries as the town dwellers. They should not be kept back in the pre-industrial revolutioners merely to act as patrons of the village artisan.

Roadmap to Cut Deficit Exists: FM

Sitting on a Treasure trove, the govt. plans to make at least 25% equity of all listed companies available to the public. Doing so in listed PSUs could help it raise thousands of crores.

Finance minister Pranab Mukherjee clarified that contrary to the general impression, he had already laid out a roadmap for reining in the fiscal deficit. Meanwhile, his officials explained why the divestment route had not been used to bridge the deficit this year — as things stand, it can't be used for that purpose, though steps would be taken to change the situation.

Officials also elaborated on the minister's promise in the Budget that the floor on non-promoter holdings in all listed companies will be hiked. The floor, they said, was likely to be set at 25%, a move that would also enable the government to justify equity sales in a whole host of PSUs.

Mukherjee said that the budgeted fiscal deficit of 6.8% of GDP for the current year was scheduled to be brought down to 5.5% next year and further to 4% in 2011–12 and he had made this explicit in the budget documents. Officials also pointed out that 6.8% was already an improvement over the effective figure for 2008–09, at 8% including bonds given to fertiliser and oil companies which are not reflected in the official deficit figures.

On the divestment issue, officials said that as things stand, all proceeds of divestment must go to the National Investment Fund (NIF) and as a result they could not be used to close the fiscal deficit or to fund expenditure on social and infrastructure sectors.

The government is now seriously considering abolishing the NIF, which was set up during the tenure of the first UPA government to counter pressure from the Left, which was opposed to disinvestment. The NIF was supposed to be used for retraining workers facing retrenchment and rehabilitating sick PSUs.

A day after the presentation of the Union Budget, a top finance ministry official said, abolishing the NIF had become important as the laid down guidelines debarred the government from funding its budget deficit using the fund's corpus. As of now, only interest component can be used.

Under the stringent rules of the NIF the government had agreed not to touch the corpus of the fund and instead use the income earned from interest for select social sector schemes, and a quarter of it for meeting capital investments in revival of PSUs.

"The NIF architecture needs to be abolished to use this money for social sector initiatives," the official said. He said the government is serious about divesting its stake in PSUs and the vision is articulated in the economic survey.

"There is very clear understanding in the government to move ahead on disinvestments," the official said, and added that it will go in for sale of equity in listed PSUs so that they have at least 25% public holding. That would create

101

enough resources for funding the government's key projects and flagship schemes, they said. Back of the envelop calculations for TOI show that if just about a dozen listed PSUs were to meet the 25% floor by disinvestment, the government could raise about Rs. 1,20,000 crore at current market prices. If the divestment happens in happier market conditions, the figure could be even higher.

www.ingramcontent.com/pod-product-compliance
Lightning Source LLC
Chambersburg PA
CBHW052045270326
41931CB00012B/2642